DISTRICT
LEADERSHIP
THAT WORKS

Striking the Right Balance

Robert J.
MARZANO

Timothy
WATERS

Solution Tree | Press

a division of

Solution Tree

Published by Solution Tree Press
555 North Morton Street
Bloomington, IN 47404
800.733.6786 (toll free) / 812.336.7700
FAX: 812.336.7790
email: info@solution-tree.com
solution-tree.com

Printed in the United States of America

12   11   10   3   4   5

FSC
Mixed Sources
Product group from well-managed
forests and other controlled sources
Cert no. SW-COC-002283
www.fsc.org
© 1996 Forest Stewardship Council

Library of Congress Cataloging-in-Publication Data

Marzano, Robert J.
  District leadership that works : striking the right balance / Robert
J. Marzano, Timothy Waters.
     p. cm.   ·
  Includes bibliographical references.
  ISBN 978-1-935249-19-1 (perfect bound) -- ISBN 978-1-935249-26-9
(library bdg.) 1. School districts--Administration. 2. Educational
leadership. I. Waters, Timothy, 1948- II. Title.
  LB2817.M364 2009
  371.2'011--dc22
                         2009006901

Solution Tree
Jeffrey C. Jones, CEO & President

Solution Tree Press
President: Douglas M. Rife
Publisher: Robert D. Clouse
Vice President of Production: Gretchen Knapp
Managing Editor of Production: Caroline Wise
Proofreader: Elisabeth Abrams
Text Designer: Amy Shock
Compositor: Raven Bongiani
Cover Designer: Orlando Angel

Acknowledgments

Solution Tree Press would like to thank the following reviewers:

Marsha Brown
Assistant Superintendent of Educational Services
Orange Unified School District
Orange, California

John Eller
Assistant Professor
Virginia Polytechnic Institute and State University
Blacksburg, Virginia

William Habermehl
County Superintendent of Schools
Orange County Department of Education
Costa Mesa, California

Theodore Kowalski
Professor
University of Dayton
Dayton, Ohio

Ann Roy Moore
Superintendent
Huntsville City Schools
Huntsville, Alabama

Eugene Tucker
Adjunct Professor
University of California at Los Angeles
Los Angeles, California

Table of Contents

About the Authors

Dr. Robert J. Marzano is cofounder and CEO of Marzano Research Laboratory in Centennial, Colorado, and senior scholar at Mid-continent Research for Education and Learning (McREL) in Denver, Colorado. He is the author of thirty books, one hundred and fifty articles and chapters in books, and one hundred sets of curriculum materials for teachers and students in grades K–12. During his forty years in public education, Dr. Marzano has worked in every state and in many countries in Europe and Asia. The central theme in his work has been translating research and theory into practical programs and tools for K–12 teachers and administrators.

His works include: *The Art and Science of Teaching, Classroom Assessment and Grading That Work, What Works in Schools, School Leadership That Works, Building Background Knowledge for Academic Achievement, Classroom Management That Works, Classroom Instruction That Works, Transforming Classroom Grading,* and *A Different Kind of Classroom.*

Dr. J. Timothy (Tim) Waters has served as president and CEO for McREL since 1993. In his twenty-three years in the K–12 system, serving as a superintendent, assistant superintendent, high school principal, assistant principal, and teacher, Dr. Waters established a reputation as an innovator and leader of education improvement and reform. Dr. Waters has authored numerous articles on the subject of educational leadership and is coauthor of *School Leadership That Works.* He has served on the board of directors of the Council of Educational Development and Research, the board of the National Education Knowledge Industry Association, the National Policy Board for Educational Administration research panel, and the American Association of School Administrators Institute for Leadership Networks advisory panel. Dr. Waters speaks nationally and internationally on the topic of leadership and the future of education. He received his BA from the University of Denver and his MA and Ed.D. from Arizona State University.

1 Does District Leadership Matter?

In his state of education address in 1987, Secretary of Education William Bennett attached the nickname "the blob" to administrators and the administrative system in public schools. The blob, he argued, is made up of people in the education system who work outside of classrooms, soaking up resources and resisting reform without contributing to student achievement (Walker, 1987). According to Bennett, the term *blob* is an acronym for "bloated educational bureaucracy." Those who are science fiction aficionados might also make a connection to the 1958 sci-fi movie *The Blob* starring Steve McQueen and the 1988 remake starring Kevin Dillon. For those who are not, the blob was an amorphous mass from outer space that assimilated all living tissue in its path. Those organisms unlucky enough to be assimilated by the blob ceased to exist as independent entities. Rather, they existed only as a source of nutrients for the blob. Whether or not Bennett intended the allusion to the other-worldly blob, the moniker was not a complimentary one for school administrators and the administrative system.

Bennett and his coauthors (Bennett, Finn, & Cribb, 1999) reiterated this allusion in *The Educated Child* when they wrote,

> The public school establishment is one of the most stubbornly intransigent forces on the planet. It is full of people and organizations dedicated to protecting established programs and keeping things just the way they are. Administrators talk of reform even as they are circling the wagons to fend off change, or preparing to outflank your innovation . . . To understand many of the problems besetting U.S. schools, it is necessary to know something about the education establishment christened the "blob" by one of the authors. (p. 628)

Apparently, the blob cuts a wide swath since Bennett et al. (1999) include superintendents, district office staff, and local school board members as members of the amorphous mass. Certainly, one can find examples of local school district bureaucracies that stand in the way of efforts to improve K–12 schooling. But does this characterization apply to administration in general? Is district administration really unrelated to student

1

learning (at best) or detrimental to student learning (at worst)? These were precisely the questions we set out to answer by examining the extant research on the relationship between district administrative leadership and student achievement.

To put the study described in this book in perspective, consider a similar study we completed regarding the effect of leadership at the school level (that is, leadership by building principals). We reported our findings in a book titled *School Leadership That Works: From Research to Results* (Marzano, Waters, & McNulty, 2005). There, we concluded that principal leadership has a correlation of .25 with average student achievement in a school. One way to interpret this finding is that the actions of the principal in a school have a moderate but significant relationship with average student achievement in the school (see Technical Note 1.1, page 117, for a more detailed interpretation). Certain behaviors on the part of the principal influence policy in the school, the behaviors of the teachers, and maybe even the behavior of the students. While one might argue that the actions of a principal do not directly affect or "cause" student achievement since principals do not actually work with students on a daily basis, a more balanced and reasonable interpretation (we believe) is that the actions of the principal are an important part of the mix of activities that in the aggregate have a powerful causal effect on student achievement.

The study described in this book sought to determine whether leadership at the district level has a similar relationship with student achievement—whether it is an important part of the mix of actions that in the aggregate have a causal effect on student achievement. The answer is not obvious. As indicated by the preceding discussion, there are those who believe that the actions of district-level administrators have little or no relationship with student achievement. If this is the case, then the job of district-level administrators should be limited to supporting the decisions made at the school level and "staying out of the way" of effective schooling. However, if there is a discernable relationship between district leadership and student achievement, then a proactive stance would be warranted—a stance that calls district administrators to provide strong guidance and maybe even mandates regarding what occurs in the classrooms throughout the district. Consequently, our study sought to answer two basic questions:

1. What is the strength of relationship between district-level administrative actions and average student achievement?

2. What are the specific district leadership behaviors that are associated with student achievement?

The Study

The methodology we used for our study is meta-analysis. The specifics of meta-analysis are detailed in a number of works (see Cooper & Hedges, 1994; Hunter & Schmidt, 2004; Lipsey & Wilson, 2001). In brief, meta-analysis involves a range of quantitative techniques for synthesizing research regarding a specific topic. In this case, that topic is school district leadership.

As in our previous study of school leadership, we undertook a type of meta-analysis that seeks to uncover the true underlying relationship between district leadership and student achievement. Such an approach to meta-analysis is articulated by Hunter and Schmidt (2004). Fundamentally, this type of analysis goes beyond simply synthesizing the findings of a set of studies to aggregate their effects. In fact, the latter is a more common form of meta-analysis—simply attempting to quantitatively summarize previous studies. Hunter and Schmidt offer an alternate purpose for meta-analysis that ultimately provides more guidance for practitioners:

> Our view of the purpose of meta-analysis is different: The purpose is to estimate as accurately as possible the construct-level relationships in the population (i.e., to estimate population values or parameters), because these are the relationships of scientific interest. This is an entirely different task; this is the task of estimating what the findings would have been if all the studies had been conducted perfectly (i.e., with no methodological limitations). Doing this requires correction for sampling error, measurement error, and other artifacts (when present) that distort study results. Simply quantitatively summarizing and describing the contents of studies in the literature requires no such corrections and does not allow estimation of parameters of scientific interest. (pp. 512–513)

In general, we used the Hunter and Schmidt perspective to obtain the most accurate representation of the relationship between district-level leadership and student achievement. (For a more detailed discussion of the methodology we employed, see Technical Note 1.2, page 118.)

The targeted sample for our meta-analysis was all available studies involving district leadership (or variables related to district leadership) and student academic achievement in the United States from 1970 until 2005. All studies possessed the following characteristics:

- Reported a correlation between district leadership or district leadership variables and student academic achievement, or allowed for the computing or estimating of a correlation

- Used a standardized measure of student achievement or some index based on a standardized measure of student achievement

To identify potential studies that met these criteria, four databases were queried—(1) ERIC, (2) PsycINFO, (3) Dissertation Abstracts, and (4) the AERA online search services. Keywords employed in those searches included the following: *superintendent leadership, district leadership, effective superintendents,* and *effective districts.* In all, more than 4,500 nonrepeating titles were retrieved. Of those titles, abstracts revealed that more than two hundred retrievable documents appeared to meet the identified parameters. These documents were retrieved and examined. Of those, twenty-seven met the identified criteria. The demographics for these twenty-seven reports were as follows:

- Number of districts involved—2,714

- Estimated number of ratings of superintendent leadership—4,500

- Estimated number of student achievement scores—3.4 million

Although there was a good deal of variation in the methodologies employed, the majority of studies we examined surveyed superintendents regarding their perceptions of district-level variables. In some cases, the superintendents' perceptions were combined with those of other related constituents such as board members, school-level administrators, and teachers. These perceptual data were then correlated with average student academic achievement at the district level.

The Relationship Between District Leadership and Student Achievement

Our primary research question was the following:

- What is the strength of relationship between district-level administrative actions and average student achievement?

Of the twenty-seven reports examined in the meta-analysis, fourteen contained information about the relationship between overall district-level leadership and average student academic achievement in the district. These fourteen reports included data from 1,210 districts. The computed correlation between district leadership and student achievement was .24 and was statistically significant at the .05 level.

What Does a Correlation Tell You?

Correlations can be interpreted in a variety of ways (for a review, see Cohen, Cohen, West, & Aiken, 2003). One of the most common interpretations is to examine the expected change in the dependent variable associated with a one standard deviation gain in the independent variable (Magnusson, 1966). (See Technical Note 1.1, page 117, for this interpretation and Technical Note 1.3, page 126, for other interpretations). In this case, the independent variable is district-level leadership and the dependent variable is average student achievement in the district. To interpret the correlation of .24, consider an average superintendent; that means that he is at the 50th percentile in terms of his leadership skills. Also, assume that this superintendent is leading a district where the average student achievement is also at the 50th percentile. Now, assume that the superintendent improves his or her leadership abilities by one standard deviation (in this case, rising to the 84th percentile of all district leaders). Given the correlation between district leadership and student achievement of .24, we would predict that average student achievement in the district would increase by 9.5 percentile points. In other words, average student achievement in the district would rise to the 59.5th percentile as shown in figure 1.1.

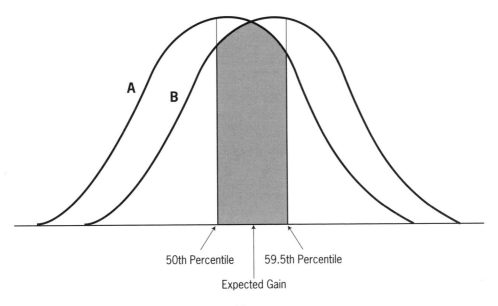

Figure 1.1 District leadership and student achievement

Curve A in figure 1.1 depicts the district at the 50th percentile in terms of average student achievement and average district-level leadership. Curve B depicts the expected average academic achievement of students in the same district after district leadership has increased in quality by one standard deviation. Again, one would predict average student academic achievement to increase from the 50th percentile to the 59.5th percentile—a gain of almost 10 percentile points.

This finding stands in sharp contrast to the notion that district administration is a part of an amorphous blob that soaks up valuable resources without adding value to a district's effectiveness. To the contrary, these findings suggest that when district leaders are carrying out their leadership responsibilities effectively, student achievement across the district is positively affected.

Specific Leadership Behaviors

Our second research question was the following:

- What are the specific district leadership behaviors that are associated with student achievement?

In response to this question, we found five district-level leadership "responsibilities" or "initiatives" with a statistically significant ($p < .05$) correlation with average student academic achievement (see Technical Note 1.4, page 129, for a more detailed discussion of the correlations associated with the five district-level responsibilities or initiatives). Throughout this text, we will use the terms *responsibilities* and *initiatives* interchangeably to signify specific actions in which district leadership should engage. They are as follows:

1. Ensuring collaborative goal setting

2. Establishing nonnegotiable goals for achievement and instruction

3. Creating board alignment with and support of district goals

4. Monitoring achievement and instruction goals

5. Allocating resources to support the goals for achievement and instruction

Each of these responsibilities or initiatives is described briefly here and in detail in subsequent chapters.

Ensuring Collaborative Goal Setting

Effective district leaders include all relevant stakeholders, including central office staff, building-level administrators, and board members, in establishing nonnegotiable goals for their districts. In particular, they ensure that building-level administrators (principals) throughout the district are heavily involved in the goal-setting process since these are the individuals who, for all practical purposes, will implement articulated goals in schools. Involving principals and school board members in the goal-setting process does not imply that consensus must be reached among these stakeholders. However, it does imply that once stakeholders reach an acceptable level of agreement regarding district goals, all stakeholders agree to support the attainment of those goals.

Establishing Nonnegotiable Goals for Achievement and Instruction

Effective district leaders ensure that the collaborative goal-setting process results in nonnegotiable goals (goals that all staff members must act on) in at least two areas: (1) student achievement and (2) classroom instruction. This means that the district sets specific achievement targets for the district as a whole, for individual schools, and for subpopulations of students within the district. Once agreed upon, the achievement goals are enacted in every school site. All staff members in each building are aware of the goals, and an action plan is created for those goals.

With respect to goals for classroom instruction, this responsibility *does not* mean that the district establishes a single instructional model that all teachers must employ. However, it *does* mean that the district adopts a broad but common framework for classroom instructional design and planning that guarantees the consistent use of research-based instructional strategies in each school.

Another characteristic of this responsibility is that all principals support district goals *explicitly* and *implicitly*. Explicit support means that school leaders engage in the behaviors in the preceding description. Implicit support means that building-level administrators do nothing to subvert the accomplishment of those goals such as criticizing district goals or subtly communicating that the goals the district has selected are inappropriate or unattainable.

Creating Board Alignment With and Support of District Goals

In effective districts, the local board of education is aligned with and supportive of the nonnegotiable goals for achievement and instruction. The board ensures that these goals remain the top priorities in the district and that no other initiatives deflect attention or resources from accomplishing these goals. Although other initiatives might be undertaken, they must directly relate to these two primary goals. Indeed, publicly adopting broad five-year goals for achievement and instruction and consistently supporting these goals, both publicly and privately, are precisely the board-level actions that are most directly related to student achievement.

It is not unusual that individual board members pursue their own interests and expectations for the districts they are elected to serve. Our findings suggest, however, that individual board members are not contributing to district success, but, in fact, may be working in opposition to that end when their interests and expectations distract attention from board-adopted achievement and instructional goals.

Monitoring Achievement and Instruction Goals

Effective superintendents continually monitor district progress toward achievement and instructional goals to ensure that these goals remain the driving force behind the district's actions. If not monitored continually, district goals can become little more than pithy refrains that are spoken at district and school events and highlighted in written reports. Effective superintendents ensure that each school regularly examines the extent to which it is meeting achievement targets. Discrepancies between articulated goals and current practices are interpreted as a need to change or to redouble efforts to enhance student achievement. In short, each school uses the achievement goals as the primary indicator of their success. The same can be said for instructional goals. Any discrepancies between expected teacher behavior in classrooms as articulated by agreed-upon instructional models and observed teacher behavior are taken as a call for corrective action.

Allocating Resources to Support the Goals for Achievement and Instruction

High-performing districts ensure that the necessary resources, including time, money, personnel, and materials, are allocated to accomplish the district's goals. This can mean cutting back on or dropping initiatives that are not aligned with district goals for achievement and instruction. Our analysis does not answer questions about the level of resources school districts must commit to supporting district achievement and instructional goals. However, it is clear from our analysis that a meaningful commitment of funding must be dedicated to professional development for teachers *and* principals. The professional development supported with this funding should be focused on building the requisite knowledge, skills, and competencies teachers and principals need to accomplish district goals. Furthermore, as professional development resources are deployed at the school level, they must be used in ways that align schools with district goals.

A Surprising and Perplexing Finding: Defined Autonomy

One set of findings from our meta-analysis that at first appears contradictory involves building-level autonomy within a district. One study reported that building autonomy has a positive correlation of .28 with average student achievement in the district, indicating that an increase in building autonomy is associated with an *increase* in student achievement (see Technical Note 1.5, page 131, for a more detailed discussion). Interestingly, that same study reported that site-based management has a negative correlation with student achievement of (−) .16, indicating that an increase in site-based management is associated with a *decrease* in student achievement.

Other studies on site-based management reported slightly better results. However, the average correlation between site-based management and student achievement was (for all practical purposes) 0.0. How can we find school autonomy positively correlated with student achievement and site-based management exhibiting a negligible or negative correlation with achievement? This question might be answered in light of our other findings. The superintendent who implements an inclusive goal-setting process that results in board-adopted "nonnegotiable goals for achievement and instruction," who assures that schools align their use of district resources for professional development with district goals, and who monitors and evaluates progress toward goal achievement is fulfilling multiple responsibilities associated with high levels of achievement. This superintendent has established a relationship with schools we refer to as *defined autonomy* when he or she also encourages principals and others to assume responsibility for school success. *Defined autonomy* means that the superintendent expects building principals and all other administrators in the district to lead *within the boundaries defined by the district goals.*

Superintendents in districts large enough to employ assistant superintendents, directors, and other administrative staff members will quickly recognize the implications of this finding for their district office staff. In most large districts, superintendents fulfill responsibilities for planning, goal adoption, board alignment and support, resource alignment, and monitoring primarily through the district office staff. District-level leadership contributes positively to student achievement when an understanding of defined autonomy is shared and honored by all district office personnel. District office staff may very well resemble what Bennett labeled the "blob" when they are unable or unwilling to support each school's defined autonomy (Walker, 1987).

The "Bonus" Finding

Our meta-analysis produced one finding that initially was not a focus of the study, but serendipitously emerged from the analysis of the reports in our study. Two studies that we examined reported correlations between superintendent tenure and student academic achievement. The weighted average correlation from these two studies was .19 significant at the .05 level (see Technical Note 1.6, page 132, for a more detailed discussion).

This finding is noteworthy in light of the discussion in the introductory section regarding the alleged lack of impact on student achievement attributed to the blob. Specifically, this finding implies that the longevity of the superintendent has a positive effect on the average academic achievement of students in the district. This positive effect may manifest itself as early as two years into a superintendent's tenure.

The District, Schools, and Teachers Working Together

The perspective on district leadership in the preceding description is a compelling one in terms of the potential importance of sound district-level leadership. Additionally, we were able to combine the findings from our meta-analysis of the research on district leadership with other research to construct a mathematical model of how district leadership, school leadership, and teacher behavior might interact to affect individual student achievement. This is depicted in tables 1.1 and 1.2 (page 10).

Tables 1.1 and 1.2 depict the predicted effects on student achievement in reading and mathematics of differing levels of leadership and competence at the district level, school level, and teacher level. Before discussing these figures, it is important to note that the figures are based on a mathematical model using our research and that of others (see Technical Note 1.7, page 132, for a discussion of how these figures were constructed). Mathematical models at best are attempts to depict what occurs in specific situations. They are not precise depictions of reality. This sentiment is credited to famous mathematical statistician George Box who is reported to have said that all mathematical models are false but some are useful (de Leeuw, 2004). With this in mind, it is instructive to examine the pattern of findings reported in tables 1.1 and 1.2. We begin with table 1.1.

Table 1.1 Effects of District, School, and Teacher on Reading Achievement

District	School	Teacher	Predicted Achievement Gain for 50th Percentile Student
Average (50th percentile)	Average (50th percentile)	Average (50th percentile)	0
Average (50th percentile)	Average (50th percentile)	Superior (84th percentile)	10
Average (50th percentile)	Average (50th percentile)	Excellent (98th percentile)	20
Superior (84th percentile)	Superior (84th percentile)	Average (50th percentile)	7
Excellent (98th percentile)	Excellent (98th percentile)	Average (50th percentile)	13

Table 1.2 Effects of District, School, and Teacher on Mathematics Achievement

District	School	Teacher	Predicted Achievement Gain for 50th Percentile Student
Average (50th percentile)	Average (50th percentile)	Average (50th percentile)	0
Average (50th percentile)	Average (50th percentile)	Superior (84th percentile)	14
Average (50th percentile)	Average (50th percentile)	Excellent (98th percentile)	26
Superior (84th percentile)	Superior (84th percentile)	Average (50th percentile)	9
Excellent (98th percentile)	Excellent (98th percentile)	Average (50th percentile)	17

The columns in table 1.1 are labeled *district, school, teacher,* and *student.* Consider the first row that contains the descriptor *average* (50th percentile) for the district, school, and teacher. As indicated, *average* is operationally defined as performance at the 50th percentile. Consider what this means for the district entry. According to the National Center for Education Statistics (NCES, 2008), there are about 14,200 districts in the United States. If these districts were ordered in terms of the effectiveness of their leadership at the central office, it is reasonable to assume that they would form a normal distribution. In table 1.1, we are defining an average district as one that is close to or right at the 50th percentile on that distribution. The same might be said for schools. There are about 97,000 K–12 schools (NCES, 2008). They too would form a normal distribution if ordered in terms of the leadership at the school level. An average school would be one at or near the 50th percentile in terms of its leadership. Finally, there are about 3.3 million teachers in the United States (NCES, 2008). They too would form a normal distribution if ordered in terms of their pedagogical competence. Again, we are defining an average teacher as one at or near the 50th percentile in terms of this distribution. The last column in table 1.1 depicts the predicted achievement gain of a student who starts at the 50th percentile. Examining the first row of table 1.1, we see that no gain is predicted when the district, the school, and the teacher are all at the 50th percentile and remain in this position; the student who begins at the 50th percentile is predicted to stay at the 50th percentile.

Now consider the second row in table 1.1. Here, the district and school rankings remain the same (average), but the teacher has risen to the status of superior. *Superior* is defined as being at the 84th percentile in terms of pedagogical competence. In this case, the mathematical model predicts that the student who begins at the 50th percentile will increase his or her achievement in reading 10 percentile points—he or she will move from the 50th to the 60th percentile. The third row depicts a more dramatic change in teacher competence and a subsequently more dramatic change in student achievement. Here, the teacher is classified as *excellent*, which is operationally defined as being at the 98th percentile in pedagogical competence. In this case, one would anticipate a gain of 20 percentile points in reading achievement—the student would move from the 50th to the 70th percentile. The inference from these figures is straightforward. The more competent the teacher, the greater the expected gain in student achievement.

Rows 2 and 3 of table 1.1 hold the district and school competence at the same level—average. Rows 4 and 5 of table 1.1 examine expected gain in student achievement if teacher competence is held constant at average while district and school leadership increase to superior and excellent. In row 4, both the district and school are classified as superior. They are at the 84th percentile in terms of their leadership. The anticipated gain in student achievement is 7 percentile points. A student is expected to move from the 50th to the 57th percentile. The fifth row again holds the teacher at the 50th percentile but moves the district and school to the excellent category—the 98th percentile. Here, the expected achievement gain for students is 13 percentile points. A student at the 50th percentile would be expected to move to the 63rd percentile. Similar patterns are depicted in table 1.2 for mathematics.

Again, the findings in tables 1.1 and 1.2 are based on mathematical models that attempt to mirror reality. As such, they should be interpreted with caution. However, the patterns illustrated in tables 1.1 and 1.2 portray an interesting possibility. Effective leadership behavior at the district and school levels can have a positive impact on student achievement. Of course, a logical question is how can actions on the part of the district and school influence student achievement when the teacher is the one interacting with students in the classroom? The findings from our meta-analysis provide a plausible explanation. Effective leadership at the district and school levels changes what occurs in classrooms, and what happens in classrooms has a direct effect on student achievement. In subsequent chapters, we will examine how district- and school-level leadership behaviors interact to affect the classroom teacher in such a way as to enhance student achievement.

Summary

In this chapter, we provided a brief overview of the findings of our meta-analyses of the research on district leadership. Contrary to the opinion that district leadership has no relationship to student achievement or is an impediment to student achievement, our findings suggest that district leadership has a measurable effect on student achievement. Additionally, five district-level responsibilities or initiatives were identified as follows: (1) ensuring collaborative goal setting, (2) establishing nonnegotiable goals for achievement and instruction, (3) creating board alignment with and support of district goals, (4) monitoring achievement and instruction goals, and (5) allocating resources to support the goals for achievement and instruction. This chapter also reported the findings from a mathematical model derived from the research on the relative effects of districts, schools, and teachers. That model predicts that when districts and schools are high functioning in terms of their leadership behaviors, they can positively influence student achievement. This is most probably because high-functioning districts and schools influence what happens in the classroom, which, in turn, influences student achievement.

2 Putting Our Findings in Perspective

The findings reported in chapter 1 imply new hope for and a new view of district leadership—one that assumes district leadership can be a critical component of effective schooling. Under this new view, district leaders should adopt a proactive stance that ensures certain uniform behaviors occur in every school in every classroom. This stands in contrast to what we believe is the current perspective that district leadership should allow schools to operate as independent entities and allow the teachers within those units to operate as independent contractors. This perspective has been driven by the theory that districts and schools are by definition loosely coupled systems.

Districts and Schools as Loosely Coupled Systems

In a series of articles, Karl Weick (1976, 1982) set the stage for what is arguably the reigning view of districts and schools as administrative units. Drawing on general organizational theory (such as Glassman, 1973), he made the distinction between tightly coupled and loosely coupled organizations. He noted that tightly coupled organizations have four defining characteristics:

1. They are self-correcting rational systems with highly interdependent components.

2. They have consensus on goals and the means to accomplish those goals.

3. They can coordinate activity by disseminating information.

4. They have predictable problems and the means to address those problems.

Given these defining characteristics, Weick (1982) concluded that educational systems (districts and schools) by nature are not tightly coupled (that is, they are loosely coupled). Relative to the characteristic of interdependent components, he noted that districts and schools are "joined more loosely than is true for other organizations" (p. 673). To illustrate, in tightly coupled systems, a poorly performing individual attracts attention. In response, performance of the individual is brought up to an acceptable level or the individual is replaced since his or her behavior is jeopardizing the effectiveness of the entire system. In contrast, Weick provided the following example drawn from schools:

> For example, only a limited amount of inspection and evaluation occurs in schools. A principal who visits a classroom too frequently is accused of "harassment." Professionals are reluctant to give one another unsolicited feedback. As a result, poor performance persists because inattention is justified as respect for professional autonomy. (1982, p. 673)

Relative to the second characteristic of tightly coupled systems—consensus on goals and the means to achieve those goals—Weick explained that districts and schools are lacking the underlying structure to exhibit this behavior:

> The goals in education are also intermediate, which makes them difficult to use as hard standards to use to evaluate individual performance. Administrators and instructors work on variable raw material with little control over the supply; they have no firm standards by which to judge the impact of their work and no clear theory of causation that specifies the effects of the things they do. (1982, p. 673)

Relative to the third characteristic of tightly coupled systems (they can coordinate activity by disseminating information), Weick argued that the cellular structure of schools and classrooms works against individual teachers and administrators having a holistic perspective of the organization. Thus, information about the functioning of the organization as a whole has little impact on behavior of individuals within the system:

> Ties among people are also loosened because few participants are constantly involved in everything that happens in a school [or district]. (1982, p. 673)

Finally, regarding the fourth characteristic of predictable problems and the means to address those problems, Weick explained,

> There are few employees and many students. Teachers find it hard to keep track of the students, let alone of one another. Since the technology of education is not clear, educators try many different things and find it difficult to tell what works. (1982, p. 673)

Given Weick's analysis of districts and schools, it is no wonder that he concluded they are loosely coupled by nature. Interestingly, he argued that not all aspects of districts and schools are loosely coupled. Indeed, some aspects are fairly tightly coupled. As examples, he used bus schedules and payroll:

> The bus schedule, for example, . . . [is] tightly coupled. Students and drivers know where people are supposed to be and whether and when buses are running late or early . . . How people get paid is tightly

coupled. When the payroll clerk fouls up, the system grinds to a halt, people raise their voices, and something gets done fast. (1982, p. 673)

Bus schedules and payroll notwithstanding, Weick's analysis leads one to the conclusion that districts and schools are, and probably will always be, loosely coupled when it comes to student achievement and classroom instruction. Once one accepts this position, one also concedes any possibility of districts and schools having a systematic positive effect on student achievement. Rather, districts and the schools within them must be thought of as populated by independent contractors (that is, teachers) each with their own view of schooling and each with their own agenda. As Weick explained, "Goals exist in loosely coupled systems, but they are tailored to local circumstances. Thus different people have different goals" (1982, p. 676).

We contend that Weick's position has unwittingly become the accepted mode of operation in U.S. districts and schools. Recent initiatives support our contention. One of these initiatives is site-based management.

Issues With Site-Based Management

Site-based management can be considered a logical and perhaps necessary administrative structure if one assumes that loose coupling is a defining feature of U.S. districts and schools. Site-based management (also known as school-based management) is not a new phenomenon. As Malen, Ogawa, and Kranz (1990b) note, calls for site-based management typically have occurred as a reaction to a perception that current problems are diverse and difficult:

> The documentary data suggest that these initiatives tend to surface during periods of intense stress . . . when, in sum, a turbulent environment generates a host of highly salient demands and the system is pressed for solutions to a cluster of seemingly intractable problems. (p. 297)

At the heart of site-based management is the distribution of decision-making authority. Typically within site-based management approaches, there is great latitude in terms of who makes decisions and the types of decisions that are made. In some instances, the principal is the focal point of decision-making power. In others, decision-making power is spread equally among all relevant constituent groups including teachers and parents.

Even though site-based management comes in many forms, all have some common characteristics. Malen, Ogawa, and Kranz (1990b) note,

> While there are different definitions of the term, school-based management can be viewed conceptually as a formal alteration of governance structures, as a form of decentralization that identifies the individual school as the primary unit of improvement and relies on redistribution

of decision making authority as the primary means through which improvements might be stimulated and sustained. (p. 290)

Miller (1995) explains that the site-based management movement received a powerful endorsement when the Carnegie Forum on Education and the Economy and the Holmes Group advocated decentralization of control of public schools and the empowerment of teachers. Since then, it has been consistently held up as a powerful form of school reform. About site-based management, David (1996) says, "Site-based management may be the most significant reform of the decade—a potential force for empowering educators and communities. Yet no two people agree on what it is, how to do it, or even why to do it" (p. 4). At the time David made her comments, many states were mandating some form of site-based management. For example, Kentucky required virtually every school to have a site-based council with three teachers, two parents, and the principal; Maryland and Texas required schools to have school-based decision-making teams but did not specify their constitution (David, 1996).

Anecdotal evidence suggests that site-based management has positively affected student achievement. For example, Sampson (1999) sent out questionnaires to a representative sample of superintendents in the United States and found the majority believed that the site-based management had a positive effect on student achievement. However, no data on student achievement were collected. Several position papers and project description reports credit school-based management for student achievement gain (Parker, 1979; Forum, 1988; Board of Education of the City of New York, 1987/1988; Sickler, 1988; Thomas, 1980).

This anecdotal evidence notwithstanding, a good number of researchers assert that there is little empirical evidence supporting the effect of site-based management on student achievement. A study by Jenkins, Ronk, Schrag, Rude, and Stowitschek (1994) is fairly characteristic of the findings from empirical studies that examine the relationship between site-based management and student achievement. The study involved twenty-two elementary schools, twelve in the experimental condition and ten in the control condition. Experimental schools used a site-based management approach to design more effective instructional programs. Students who were the focus of the study were special education students who were enrolled in general education classes for more than 50% of the day. Student achievement was measured using a standardized achievement test. Teacher perceptions of the change process were measured using a questionnaire. Jenkins et al. (1994) summarize the results of the study in the following way:

> Results indicated that the intervention program resulted in positive teacher attitudes toward the change process, in new approaches to organizing instruction, and in more mainstreamed instruction. However, we observed no treatment effects on students' achievement and behavior. (p. 357)

In their article "Site-Based Management: Unfulfilled Promises," Malen, Ogawa, and Kranz (1990a) examined two hundred documents on site-based management. They found eight studies that provided interpretable data as to its effectiveness. Regarding the effect of site-based management on student achievement, they concluded,

> Yet again there is little evidence that site-based management improves student achievement. Although some documents claim site-based management produces improved scores on achievement tests the requirements for making these claims are not met. (p. 56)

They further reported that the studies they examined indicated that site-based management did not appear to attain many nonachievement goals commonly credited to the approach. These include the following:

- Enabling site participants to exert substantial influence on school policy decisions

- Enhancing employee morale and motivation

- Enhancing the quality of the planning process

- Stimulating the quality of the planning process

- Stimulating instructional improvement

In a subsequent report, Malen, Ogawa, and Kranz (1990b) summarized their findings regarding site-based management in the following way:

> There is little evidence that school-based management produces substantial or sustainable improvements in either the attitudes of administrators and teachers or the instructional components of schools (p. 321). . . . There is little evidence that school-based management improves student achievement. (p. 323)

Commenting on a five-year comparative study of the effects of decentralized decision making (see Cambone, Weiss, & Wyeth, 1992; Weiss, 1995), Miller (1995) notes that contrary to the general impression that decentralizing renders schooling more efficient because teachers are less likely to be concerned with bureaucratic details, it might impede teachers from making decisions that would enhance teaching. Miller paraphrases the comments of Carol Weiss, one of the primary researchers in the study, as follows: "Teachers are likely to resist decisions that require them to make drastic changes in the way they teach" (in Miller, 1995, p. 3). Furthermore, Weiss notes that teachers have trouble seeing the big picture regarding what is best for the entire school and tend to focus on the world of their own classrooms.

Evans (1994) makes an interesting observation on site-based management. In a study of perceptions of the extent to which a district is centralized as opposed to decentralized, Evans found that while 75% of principals and central office administrators perceived their districts as highly centralized, in actuality, they were not. Rather, districts were typically an amalgam of very different decision-making structures depending on the type of decision made and the circumstances of the decision. It might be the case that district personnel who perceive their districts as highly centralized view site-based management as a cure for their ills. However, their districts might not be as centralized as they perceive, and consequently, the proposed cure offers little relief.

Finally, Baker and LeTendre (2005) provide an international perspective on site-based management. They compare the levels of decentralization in thirty-nine countries that were involved in the Trends in International Mathematics and Science Study (TIMSS) and note that "decentralization comes at a cost of less curricular consistency among a nation's classrooms" (p. 140). Of the thirty-nine countries they compared, the United States was the most decentralized:

> The federal government in the United States has little formal control over educational administration and policy. With its fifty separate state departments of education and approximately fourteen thousand semi-autonomous school districts, it is one of the most localized systems in the world today . . . Over time, this has led to a largely unplanned, but highly legitimated, public administrative system of schooling that some refer to as ultradecentralized. (p. 141)

The Call for Tight Coupling Regarding Achievement and Instruction

The preceding discussion might read as an argument against any form of control at the school level. This is certainly not our intent. Recall the surprise finding from our study regarding defined autonomy. Where studies we analyzed suggest that the overall correlation between site-based management and student achievement is close to zero, at least one study reported positive effects for school autonomy. As briefly described in chapter 1, we reconcile this apparent contradiction with the concept of defined autonomy. Schools within a district should have autonomy in terms of many aspects of their daily functioning. This might include scheduling, selecting textbooks, and determining how assessments are structured and used, to name a few. But this autonomy does not extend to renegotiating or ignoring nonnegotiable goals that have been established at the district level regarding achievement and instruction.

Our findings clearly point to the efficacy of tight coupling regarding achievement and instruction at the district level. Although the districts in the studies we analyzed most certainly differed in how they approached these two elements and the extent to which they achieved tight coupling, tight coupling clearly appears to hold great promise as the necessary ingredient for a district-level effect on student achievement. Our conclusion that tightly coupled districts can have a positive effect on student achievement is supported by a variety of sources. Next, we consider two of those sources.

The Evidence From High-Reliability Organizations

Bellamy, Crawford, Marshall, and Coulter (2005) assert that the No Child Left Behind (NCLB) Act of 2001 changed the landscape of K–12 education in that it made districts and schools accountable for student achievement probably for the first time in the history of U.S. education. Meyer and Rowan (1978) once characterized K–12 as accountable only for maintaining the social expectations that schools provide students with experiences similar to those of their parents. As Bellamy and colleagues put it (Bellamy et al., 2005), districts and schools have historically sought to "sustain social legitimacy by conforming appearances to public expectations" (p. 383). However, NCLB altered this perspective. Bellamy and colleagues note,

> The stakes for failure have been raised so high . . . that *high reliability* has become an important aspect of school success. Schools are now challenged to prevent practically all failures and to close achievement among student groups—in short, to ensure highly reliable learning for all students. (p. 384)

There are a number of salient examples of high-reliability organizations (HROs), among them electric power grids, commercial aircraft maintenance, air traffic control systems, and nuclear power plants. For organizations such as these, "the public expects fail-safe performance and successful organizations adjust their operations to prevent failure" (Bellamy et al., 2005, p. 385).

Unfortunately, all of the examples of HROs offered by Bellamy and colleagues are far removed from education. However, they do provide insight regarding how to transform districts and schools into high-reliability organizations. They list the following characteristics of HROs: (1) clear goals and constant monitoring of the extent to which goals are being met, (2) an understanding of the necessary conditions under which these goals are met, and (3) immediate corrective action when goals are not being met. To illustrate these characteristics, consider one of the examples in the preceding list. Electric power grids have clear goals regarding how much electric power must be produced for specific areas. Electrical output is monitored on a moment-by-moment basis. There is a clear understanding as to how the power grid produces electrical energy. Immediate action is taken relative to the necessary conditions to correct the error when goals are not met.

What do the characteristics of HROs identified by Bellamy et al. (2005) imply for districts and schools seeking to approach high-reliability status? In effect, if student achievement is the criterion for district and school success, and if effective teaching is a necessary condition to this end, then the work of districts and schools is quite clear. Concrete and specific achievement goals must be established and monitored. So, too, must clear goals be established and monitored for effective teaching in every classroom. Any perturbations in student achievement should signal a need to shore up instruction in classrooms.

We believe the need for districts to strive for high-reliability status is clear, as are the defining characteristics of high-reliability districts. What is not clear is whether districts have the requisite resolve to reach this status. Interestingly, Weick and his colleagues (Weick, Sutcliffe, & Obstfeld, 1999) characterized HROs as "exotic outliers in mainstream organizational theory" (p. 81). One might conclude from their remarks that the authors have a dim view of the possibility of districts and schools becoming highly reliable. We take a more optimistic view, as do Bellamy and colleagues. While they note that districts and schools might never reach the level of tight coupling exhibited by high-reliability organizations such as electric power grids, they do strongly suggest that districts and schools should continually strive for HRO status.

The Evidence From Worldwide Study of Effective Schools

The call for high-reliability districts using student achievement as the primary criterion for success and classroom instruction as the necessary condition for achievement is also supported by a recent study of effective schools worldwide conducted by the Organisation for Economic Co-operation and Development (OECD). OECD is an international organization that works with governments to address economic, social, and governance challenges. The United States is one of thirty OECD member countries. Other OECD member countries include Finland, Singapore, Australia, Canada, Belgium, Hong Kong, Japan, Netherlands, New Zealand, and South Korea.

OECD members periodically participate in the Program for International Student Assessment (PISA), which tests fifteen-year-olds on their ability to apply what they have learned in the areas of math and science. According to McKinsey and Company (2007), some assessment experts view the PISA as the most accurate measure of the education system effectiveness. It assesses both student mastery of math and science knowledge and the ability to apply knowledge to novel but relevant problems.

Following the administration of the PISA in 2003, McKinsey and Company was engaged to study the ten best-performing school systems in the world based on the results of this assessment. The ten highest-performing education systems in the world, based on PISA results, are found in the countries listed in the first paragraph. The purpose of the McKinsey study was to discover why the world's top-performing school systems perform so very much better than most others and why some educational reforms succeed so spectacularly, when most others fail (McKinsey & Company, 2007).

In their report *How the World's Best-Performing School Systems Come Out on Top*, McKinsey and Company (2007) conclude "three things matter most: 1) getting the right people to become teachers, 2) developing them into effective instructors, 3) ensuring that the system is able to deliver the best possible instruction for every child" (p. 2). The report goes on to state:

> The top performing school systems recognize that the only way to improve outcomes is to improve instruction . . . which interventions are effective in achieving this—coaching classroom practice, moving teacher training to the classroom, developing stronger school leaders, and enabling teachers to learn from each other—and have found ways to deliver these interventions throughout their school system. (p. 26)

In our terminology, the highest-performing systems in the world establish and accomplish nonnegotiable goals for instruction in every classroom, which automatically translates into enhanced academic achievement for students. These systems are able to decrease the pedagogical variability between teachers and increase the quality of instruction within schools and between schools. They do this by establishing clear instructional priorities at the system level, establishing a systematic and systemwide approach to instruction, investing in teacher preparation and professional development, and developing strong instructional leadership. Indeed, one of the final conclusions in the McKinsey and Company report states, "There is not a single documented case of a school successfully turning around its pupil achievement trajectory in the absence of talented leadership. Similarly, we did not find a single school system which had been turned around that did not possess sustained, committed, and talented leadership" (2007, p. 38).

This final conclusion is not only consistent with our findings on the importance of school- and district-level leadership but also reflects the essence of balanced leadership in HROs. Nonnegotiable instructional goals are established at the system level. These goals are supported by leadership at every level of the system. Resources are dedicated to professional development that ensures high-quality instruction, strong and knowledgeable instructional leadership, ongoing monitoring of instructional quality, and the impact of instruction on learning. Despite this tight coupling, there is sufficient autonomy and flexibility at the school level to respond quickly and effectively to early indications of error and individual student failure. Based on the McKinsey and Company study, we believe that the ten best-performing school districts in the world, as measured by the PISA, are exemplars of the leadership responsibilities and practices reported here and in our book *School Leadership That Works* (Marzano et al., 2005).

A New View of District Leadership

Recall from chapter 1 that we reported five basic findings from our analysis of the research on district leadership:

1. Ensuring collaborative goal setting

2. Establishing nonnegotiable goals for achievement and instruction

3. Creating board alignment with and support of district goals

4. Monitoring achievement and instruction goals

5. Allocating resources to support the goals for achievement and instruction

The research, theory, and informed opinions of ourselves and others put these findings in sharp focus and suggest a new way of leading districts.

- First, nonnegotiable district goals should be established for student achievement and for effective instruction, which is a necessary condition for student achievement. These goals should be monitored and used as the basis for immediate corrective action thus moving districts toward the ideal of high-reliability organizations.

- Second, the nonnegotiable goals for achievement and instruction should be established through a collaborative goal-setting process that involves key stakeholders. The board should be fully behind the nonnegotiable goals, and all available resources in the district should be used to support these nonnegotiable goals.

This listing is not a simple renaming or reordering of our basic findings. Rather, it represents a set of concrete steps we believe districts should take. In the next chapter, we begin with a discussion of nonnegotiable goals for achievement.

Summary

This chapter put the findings reported in chapter 1 in perspective relative to a prevailing view of districts and schools. For decades, educators have assumed that districts and schools are loosely coupled by their very nature when it comes to student achievement. By definition, loosely coupled districts and schools are not focused on high student achievement systemwide. The natural consequence of loosely coupled districts and schools is to move toward site-based management. However, if one accepts the premise that districts and schools can be tightly coupled regarding student achievement, then a different view of district leadership is a logical consequence. Support for the possibility of tightly coupled districts and schools regarding student achievement is found in the research and theory on high-reliability organizations and in the research regarding the highest-performing school systems in the world.

3 Setting and Monitoring Nonnegotiable Goals for Achievement

In this chapter, we address the findings from our study involving setting nonnegotiable goals for achievement and monitoring nonnegotiable goals for achievement. In the next chapter, we address our findings regarding setting nonnegotiable goals for instruction and monitoring such goals. In effect, we have separated and recombined the following two leadership actions from our study.

1. Establishing nonnegotiable goals for achievement and instruction

2. Monitoring the nonnegotiable goals for achievement and instruction

We do this for ease of discussion. Setting and monitoring goals for achievement involve coordinated activities, as do setting and monitoring goals for instruction.

To a great extent, our findings regarding nonnegotiable goals for achievement (this chapter) and nonnegotiable goals for instruction (the next chapter) are defining features of effective district leadership in that they should be the centerpiece of a comprehensive district reform effort. Figure 3.1 (page 24) represents our perceptions of the relationship between nonnegotiable goals for achievement and instruction and the other findings from our study.

In figure 3.1, the findings regarding collaborative goal setting, board alignment, and allocation of resources are at the bottom. This indicates that they are foundational to the attainment of nonnegotiable goals for achievement and instruction. They are means to an end, not ends in themselves. Note that nonnegotiable goals for achievement are at the top of the representation. This is meant to indicate that student achievement is the ultimate and superordinate end product of district reform. Everything else is in the service of this outcome. Effective instruction is considered causal to enhanced student achievement and therefore critical to the process of district reform. It is placed immediately below nonnegotiable goals for achievement. Collaborative goal setting, board alignment, and allocation of resources are the bedrock on which the goals regarding

instruction and achievement are built. They might be considered necessary, but not sufficient conditions for effective district reform.

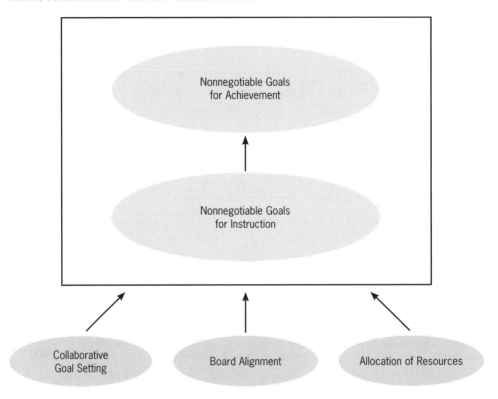

Figure 3.1 Interaction of findings for district leadership

The Context for Setting and Monitoring Nonnegotiable Goals for Achievement

Any discussion of nonnegotiable goals for achievement must address the requirements of No Child Left Behind (NCLB, 2002; much of our discussion of this issue is
drawn from Marzano, 2009).

Guilfoyle (2006) chronicles the history of NCLB and its current effects on districts
and schools. She notes that it is "the most ambitious federal education law—which pro-
poses to close achievement gaps and aims for 100 percent student proficiency by 2014"
(p. 8). From an historical perspective, NCLB is best thought of as the newest itera-
tion of the decades old Elementary and Secondary Education Act. Guilfoyle further
states, "The original law provided funding to school districts to help low-income students. Today, NCLB holds Title I schools that receive . . . federal money accountable by
requiring them to meet proficiency targets on annual assessments" (p. 8). As described
by U.S. Secretary of Education Margaret Spellings, the "linchpin" of NCLB is testing.
Guilfoyle (2006) explains,

The law requires tests in reading and math for students annually in grades 3–8 and once in high school. In 2005–2006, 23 states that had not yet fully implemented NCLB needed to administer 11.4 million new tests in reading and math. Science testing began in 2007—one test in each of three grade spans must be administered (3–5, 6–9, and 10–12)—the number of tests that states need to administer annually to comply with NCLB is expected to rise to 68 million. (p. 8)

Key to the success of NCLB or any large-scale initiative involving student achievement is an effective reporting system. Reporting systems for NCLB might be described as "status oriented" in that they reflect the proportion of students who are at specific levels of achievement on a given scale. Status-oriented reporting systems typically use summative assessments. McMillan (2007) characterizes summative assessments as "conducted mainly to monitor and record student achievement and . . . used for accountability" (p. 1). Presumably, the reason for using a status orientation as the reporting vehicle in NCLB is to provide no excuse for student failure. Regardless of the background characteristics of students, regardless of when students enter a particular school, all are expected to succeed. Theoretically, under NCLB, a district or school should seek to have 100% of students passing every test at every grade level. The sentiment behind this approach is noble but terribly unfair as a method of determining the effectiveness of a district or school for at least four reasons.

First, many districts and schools have highly transient populations. For example, some schools with whom we have worked have reported transiency rates as high as 70 percent. In other schools, reported transiency rates might be as low as 10 percent. Quite obviously, a school with a transiency rate of 10% will have more time to work with students than a school with a transiency rate of 70 percent. A status system based on summative assessments will not reflect this inequity. Typically, the proportion of students at or above a specific score on the summative assessment (commonly referred to as a "cut score" or a "performance standard") is considered the primary indicator of success for a school or district. The school with a 10% transiency rate might exhibit 85% of their students at or above the cut score, and the school with a transiency rate of 70% might exhibit 20% of their students at or above the cut score. But these differences might have little or nothing to do with the quality of education provided by the two schools. In fact, the two schools might be equal in terms of the quality of education they provide. The only difference is that one school has a highly stable population of students that allows the effects of their education system to produce easily discernable results, and the other, although equal in terms of the impact of its educational system on student achievement, simply does not have enough time to reap identifiable results because of the frequent turnover of students.

Second, districts and schools have student populations with very different demographics, and those differences are strongly related to disparities in student achievement

(Hedges & Nowell, 1999; Jacobsen, Olsen, Rice, Sweetland, & Ralph, 2001; Ladewig, 2006). Given the strong relationship between a student's family income (let's say) and student achievement, it makes sense that a district or school with a majority of students coming from high-income families will have a higher percentage of students at or above a given cut score than a district with a majority of students from low-income families. Again, this disparity might have nothing to do with the quality of the education provided. The district or school with a majority of low-income students might be superior in the education it provides, but when judged by a status-oriented assessment system that employs summative assessments, it will be perceived as inferior to its high-income counterpart.

Third, status-oriented systems based on summative assessments come with a huge price in terms of time and money. Zellmer, Frontier, and Pheifer (2006) studied this phenomenon in Wisconsin. They found that the state's summative tests required 4.75 to 8.66 hours of administration time annually for each student, amounting to 1.4 million hours of testing in the 2004–2005 school year. When NCLB testing is fully implemented, 2.9 million hours of test administration will be required. Testing requirements have a particularly dramatic effect on special populations. Because teachers are involved in test administration, special education students lose 8.5 days of instruction, 7.7, and 6.3 at the elementary, middle, and high schools, respectively. Title I students lose 8.6 days, 7.9, and 6.3 days at elementary, middle, and high schools. English language learners lose about 7.4 days of instruction. The cost of testing is also quite prohibitive. State tests cost an average of $33.91 per student. Extrapolating this cost across the 435,000 students in Wisconsin, Zellmer and colleagues estimate that Wisconsin spent $14,700,000 on NCLB-related testing.

Fourth, status systems using summative assessments provide very little information that can be used to enhance the learning of students. Indeed, the NCLB legislation is not intended to provide assessment information that can be used to inform instruction and thereby increase achievement. As Abrams (2007) explains, "It is important to note that the law [NCLB] only prescribes how schools—not students—should be held accountable" (p. 82). By definition then, NCLB is focused solely on accountability at the school level. While this approach has a legitimate logic supporting it, a more utilitarian assessment system would also provide information on individual students so that their instructional needs might be attended to.

Summative assessments come up quite short when viewed from this perspective. Cizek (2007) has demonstrated this in his analysis of a fourth-grade summative mathematics assessment from a large Midwestern state. The total score reliability for the forty items on that assessment is .87, which is acceptable by most standards. However, the test also reports subscale scores for algebra, data analysis and probability, estimation and mental computation, geometry, measurement, number and number relations, patterns, relations and functions, and problem-solving strategies. The reliabilities of these subscale scores range from .33 to .57—lower than what is typically called for when making inferences about individual students. Even more disturbingly, the reliability of the difference score is .015. Commenting on the use of data from this particular state test to make decisions about individual students, Cizek explains,

> It still might be that the dependability of conclusions about differences in subarea performance is nearly zero. In many cases, a teacher who flipped a coin to decide whether to provide the pupil with focused intervention in algebra (heads) or measurement (tails) would be making that decision about as accurately as the teacher who relied on an examination of subscore differences for the two areas. (p. 104)

In effect, large-scale status-oriented summative assessments appear to be relatively ineffective in providing information that can be used to make instructional decisions regarding individual students. For these reasons and others, Barton (2006) has called for an accountability system built on a value-added or growth model:

> If we had an accountability system that truly measured student gain— sometimes called *growth* or *value added*—we could use whether students in any year have gained enough in that school year to show adequate progress. The end goal should not be achieving set scores by 2014. The goal should be reaching a standard for *how much* growth we expect during a school year in any particular subject. (p. 30)

We agree that a value-added or growth model should be the primary type of data used by districts and states to analyze their effectiveness.

The Need for a Formatively Based, Value-Added System

In this text, we use the terms *growth*, *value added*, and *knowledge gains* interchangeably. We take the position that current advances in formative assessment make knowledge gain a viable metric.

Formative assessment has gained great popularity in recent years largely because of the findings from a comprehensive review of the literature on classroom assessment. Namely, as a result of analyzing more than 250 studies, British researchers Black and Wiliam (1998) reported the following conclusions regarding formative assessments:

> The research reported here shows conclusively that formative assessment does improve learning. The gains in achievement appear to be quite considerable, and as noted earlier, amongst the largest ever reported for educational interventions. As an illustration of just how big these gains are, an effect size of 0.7, if it could be achieved on a nationwide scale, would be equivalent to raising the mathematics attainment score of an "average" country like England, New Zealand

or the United States into the "top five" after the Pacific rim countries of Singapore, Korea, Japan and Hong Kong. (p. 61)

Based on the strength of the research on formative assessments, we recommend that districts institute a value-added approach that uses classroom formative assessments as its focal point. The model we propose here draws from previous discussions by Marzano (2006, 2007a, 2008, 2009).

A value-added approach that is based on formative assessments addresses (at least in part) all four issues brought up regarding a status-oriented approach based on summative assessments. First, the issue of different transiency rates is addressed in that a school could estimate the unique effect it had on a student's learning. Even if a student was in school for a few months only, using a formatively based system of assessment, a student's knowledge gain could be estimated. This is in sharp contrast to a status system, which merely acknowledges status at a particular point in time. Many states use a classification system with categories such as *advanced, proficient, basic,* and *below basic.* A student who is classified as basic is typically considered not meeting NCLB standards. However, that student might have entered the school a few months earlier at the status far below basic, and had, in fact, exhibited a great deal of knowledge gain as a function of the school's efforts. In a formatively based system, this gain could be documented and celebrated.

Second, a formatively based, value-added system also addresses the issue of demographics. Regardless of whether it provides high-quality or low-quality educational experiences, a school with a majority of students from higher-income homes will likely have a greater proportion of students at or above a specific proficiency level (that is, the percentage of students classified as proficient within a state classification system) than a school with a majority of students from low-income families. A value-added system would provide a very different perspective. Schools that provide low-quality educational experiences will most likely not exhibit as much knowledge gain as schools that provide high-quality educational experiences, regardless of the demographics of students in those schools.

Third, a formatively based, value-added system might even address some of the resource problems of a status system. This is because it relies on classroom-level assessments that do not detract from instructional time as do the high-stakes state-level tests that are characteristic of status approaches. Assessment data can be gleaned as a regular part of classroom instruction, as opposed to taking time away from classroom instruction as do state-level tests.

Fourth, a formatively based, value-added system addresses the characteristic inability of large-scale status systems to provide guidance regarding enhancing the achievement of individual students. This is necessarily so because formative assessments by definition focus on specific elements of information and skill and provide students with feedback regarding their progress on these elements.

Characteristics of a Formatively Based, Value-Added System

While it seems evident that a formatively based, value-added system is superior to a summatively based status system, just how to implement the former is not evident. Some districts and schools use "off the shelf" formative assessments developed by standardized test makers. In his article entitled "Phony Formative Assessments: Buyer Beware," Popham (2006) harshly criticizes the unquestioning use of commercially prepared formative assessments. He notes that:

> as news of Black and Wiliam's conclusions gradually spread into faculty lounges, test publishers suddenly began to relabel many of their tests as "formative." This name-switching sales ploy was spurred on by the growing perception among educators that formative assessments could improve their students' test scores and help their schools dodge the many accountability bullets being aimed their way. (p. 86)

He further explains that the impressive results regarding formative assessment relate to classroom assessments—those designed and administered by classroom teachers during their daily interactions with students—not to external benchmark assessments. In effect, any external assessment that is not intimately tied to day-to-day classroom practice by definition violates the tenets of formative assessment. Shepard (2006) makes the same criticism of external "formative assessments":

> The research-based concept of formative assessment, closely grounded in classroom instructional processes, has been taken over—hijacked— by commercial test publishers and is used instead to refer to formal testing systems called "benchmark" or "interim assessment systems." (as cited in Popham, 2006, p. 86)

Similar concerns have been expressed about district-made formative assessments. Specifically, they violate one basic tenet of formative assessment, which is that they must allow for both formal and informal judgments of student achievement. As McMillan (2007) explains,

> [Benchmark] assessments, which are typically provided by the district or commercial test publishers, are administered on a regular basis to compare student achievement to "benchmarks" that indicate where student performance should be in relation to what is needed to do well on end-of-year high stakes tests . . . . Although the term *benchmark* is often used interchangeably with *formative* in the commercial testing

market, there are important differences. Benchmark assessments are formal, structured tests that typically do not provide the level of detail needed for appropriate instructional correctives. (pp. 2–3)

Clearly, then, a formatively based, value-added system cannot be populated exclusively by district- or school-designed assessments, nor can it be populated by commercially prepared assessments. They simply do not satisfy the defining features of formative assessment. What, then, is necessary to develop a comprehensive system of formative assessments?

In their meta-analytic review of research on assessment, Black and Wiliam (1998) defined formative assessment in the following way: "All those activities undertaken by teachers and/or by students which provide information to be used as feedback to modify the teaching and learning activities in which they are engaged" (pp. 7–8). Wiliam and Leahy (2007) describe formative assessment as follows:

> The qualifier *formative* will refer not to an assessment or even to the purpose of an assessment, but rather to the extent that information from the assessment is fed back within the system and actually used to improve the performance of the system way (i.e., that the assessment *forms* the direction of the improvement). (p. 31)

At face value, these sentiments seem to characterize formative assessment as involving a wide array of formal and informal techniques for designing and interpreting assessments. This places the classroom teacher clearly at the center of effective formative assessment.

Drawing on the work of a number of researchers (Black & Wiliam, 1998; Fuchs & Fuchs, 1986; Wiliam & Leahy, 2007) and the specific guidance provided in *Getting Serious About School Reform* (Marzano, 2008), *Classroom Assessment and Grading That Work* (Marzano, 2006), *Making Standards Useful in the Classroom* (Marzano & Haystead, 2008), as well as other works (such as Marzano, 2007a, 2009), we have identified four phases a district would progress through to set and monitor nonnegotiable goals for achievement using a formatively based, value-added system of assessment.

Phase 1: Reconstitute State Standards as Measurement Topics or Reporting Topics

While it might not be evident initially, state standards documents as currently formatted represent a major impediment to a formatively based, value-added system of assessment. One reason is that state (and national) standards documents simply articulate too much content. To illustrate, a study conducted by researchers at Mid-continent Research for Education and Learning (McREL) found that schools and teachers need 71% more instructional time than is currently available to address the content in state and national standards (Marzano, Kendall, & Cicchinelli, 1998; Marzano, Kendall, & Gaddy, 1999).

Another critical problem with state and national standards as currently constituted is that they do not isolate measurable dimensions or traits that would allow for tracking student progress on specific elements of information and skill. Much of measurement theory is based on the assumption that an assessment for which only one score is provided representing student achievement measures a single dimension or trait (Hattie, 1984, 1985). State and national standards are not designed with this measurement principle in mind. To illustrate, consider the following science benchmark from *National Science Education Standards* (National Research Council, 1996):

- Light travels in a straight line until it strikes an object. Light can be reflected by a mirror, refracted by a lens, or absorbed by the object.

- Heat can be produced in many ways, such as burning, rubbing, or mixing one substance with another. Heat can move from one object to another by conduction.

- Electricity in circuits can produce light, heat, sound, and magnetic effects. Electrical circuits require a complete loop through which an electrical current can pass.

- Magnets attract and repel each other and certain kinds of other materials. (p. 127)

This benchmark, which is intended for grades K–4, clearly addresses multiple dimensions. Depending on how the information is presented, it might involve as many as five dimensions, one for each bullet. This example is from a national standards document. The same problem is found in state standards documents. To illustrate, consider the following fifth grade benchmark for the "measurement" standard from the Ohio state standards document entitled *Academic Content Standards: K–12 Mathematics* (Ohio Department of Education, 2001):

1. Identify and select appropriate units to measure angles; i.e., degrees.

2. Identify paths between points on a grid or coordinate plane and compare the lengths of the paths; e.g., shortest path, paths of equal length.

3. Demonstrate and describe the differences between covering the faces (surface area) and filling the interior (volume) of three-dimensional objects.

4. Demonstrate understanding of the differences among linear units, square units and cubic units.

5. Make conversions within the same measurement system while performing computations.

6. Use strategies to develop formulas for determining perimeter and area of triangles, rectangles and parallelograms, and volume of rectangular prisms.

7. Use benchmark angles (e.g., 45°, 90°, 120°) to estimate the measure of angles, and use a tool to measure and draw angles. (pp. 72–73)

Again, this single benchmark statement includes many dimensions. To remedy this situation, Marzano (Marzano, 2006; Marzano & Haystead, 2008) recommends that state documents be reconstituted in such a way that they articulate a relatively small number of measurement topics or "reporting topics" that address single dimensions or dimensions that are closely related. To illustrate, consider table 3.1, which contains sample reporting topics for language arts, mathematics, science, and social studies.

Table 3.1 Sample Measurement or Reporting Topics

Language Arts

Reading:
  1. Word recognition and vocabulary
  2. Reading comprehension
  3. Literary analysis

Writing:
  4. Spelling
  5. Language mechanics and conventions
  6. Research and technology
  7. Evaluation and revision

Listening and Speaking:
  8. Listening comprehension
  9. Analysis and evaluation of oral media
 10. Speaking applications

Mathematics

Numbers and Operations:
  1. Number sense and number systems
  2. Operations and estimation

Computation:
  3. Addition and subtraction
  4. Multiplication and division

Algebra and Functions:
  5. Patterns, relations, and functions
  6. Algebraic representations and mathematical models

Geometry:
  7. Lines, angles, and geometric objects
  8. Transformations, congruency, and similarity

Measurement: 9. Measurement systems 10. Perimeter, area, and volume
Data Analysis and Probability: 11. Data organization and interpretation 12. Probability

Science

Nature of Science:
1.   Nature of scientific knowledge and inquiry
2.   Scientific enterprise

Physical Sciences:
3.   Structure and properties of matter
4.   Sources and properties of energy
5.   Forces and motion

Life Sciences:
6.   Biological evolution and diversity of life
7.   Principles of heredity and related concepts
8.   Structure and function of cells and organisms
9.   Relationships among organisms and their physical environment

Earth and Space Sciences:
10.   Atmospheric processes and the water cycle
11.   Composition and structure of the Earth
12.   Composition and structure of the Universe and the Earth's place in it

Social Studies

Citizenship, Government, and Democracy:
1.   Rights, responsibilities, and participation in the political process
2.   The U.S. and state constitutions
3.   The civil and criminal legal systems

Culture and Cultural Diversity:
4.   The nature and influence of culture

Economics:
5.   The nature and function of economic systems
6.   Economics throughout the world
7.   Personal economics

History:
8.   Significant individuals and events
9.   Current events and the modern world

Geography:
10.   Spatial thinking and the use of charts, maps, and graphs

Note that table 3.1 lists ten language arts reporting topics (organized into three broad categories of reading, writing, and listening and speaking, sometimes referred to as *strands*), twelve mathematics topics (organized into six strands), twelve science topics (organized into four strands), and ten social studies topics (organized into five strands). By definition, the articulation of a small set of reporting topics that are unidimensional or involve closely related dimensions will allow states (or districts adapting state standards) to focus on a critical set of academic content that can actually be taught in the time available to teachers.

Once measurement topics have been identified, a scale must be constructed that is amenable to formative assessments that are sensitive to learning over time and knowledge gain. Both empirically and conceptually, Marzano (2002, 2006) has demonstrated that scoring assessments using a 100-point or percentage scale typically is not sensitive to learning over time. In lieu, he offers the scale depicted in table 3.2.

Table 3.2 Generic Scale for Design of Formative Assessments

Score 4.0	**In addition to Score 3.0 performance, in-depth inferences and applications that go beyond what was taught.**
Score 3.5	In addition to Score 3.0 performance, partial success at inferences and applications that go beyond what was taught (Score 4.0 elements).
Score 3.0	**Score 3.0: No major errors or omissions regarding any of the information and/or processes (simple or complex) that were explicitly taught.**
Score 2.5	No major errors or omissions regarding the simpler details and processes (Score 2.0 elements) and partial knowledge of the more complex ideas and processes (Score 3.0 elements).
Score 2.0	**No major errors or omissions regarding the simpler details and processes (Score 2.0 elements) but major errors or omissions regarding the more complex ideas and processes (Score 3.0 elements).**
Score 1.5	Partial knowledge of the simpler details and processes (Score 2.0 elements) but major errors or omissions regarding the more complex ideas and processes (Score 3.0 elements).
Score 1.0	**With help, a partial understanding of some of the simpler details and processes (Score 2.0 elements) and some of the more complex ideas and processes (Score 3.0 elements).**
Score 0.5	With help, a partial understanding of some of the simpler details and processes (Score 2.0 elements) but not the more complex ideas and processes (Score 3.0 elements).
Score 0.0	**Score 0.0: Even with help, no understanding or skill demonstrated.**

The scale in table 3.2 is generic and must be rewritten for specific reporting topics. Before we provide an example of a scale written for a specific topic, it is useful to consider the general characteristics of the scale. The lowest score value on the scale is a 0.0, representing no knowledge of the topic—even with help, the student demonstrates no understanding or skill relative to the topic that is being assessed. A score of 1.0 indicates that *with help,* the student shows partial knowledge of the simpler details and processes as well as the more complex ideas and processes. To be assigned a score of 2.0, the student independently demonstrates understanding of and skill at the simpler details and processes but not the more complex ideas and processes. A score of 3.0 indicates that the student demonstrates understanding of all information and skill—simple and complex—*that was taught in class.* A score of 4.0 indicates that the student demonstrates inferences and applications that *go beyond what was taught in class.* Half-point scores indicate partial credit at the next full-score level.

Using the generic scale depicted in table 3.2 as a guide, all reporting topics at every grade level can be written in the scale format. To illustrate, consider table 3.3.

Table 3.3 Scale for Biological Diversity and Evolution of Life (Grade 8)

Score 4.0	**In addition to score 3.0, in-depth inferences and applications that go beyond what was taught such as:** • describing how a genetic disorder (e.g., cystic fibrosis) can be passed from parents to offspring when the parents are healthy
Score 3.5	In addition to score 3.0 performance, in-depth inferences and applications with partial success.
Score 3.0	**While engaged in tasks that address principles of heredity, the student demonstrates an understanding of important information such as:** • distinctions between asexual and sexual reproduction (risk of mutation, energy requirements, similarity of offspring to parent, processes involved) (*e.g., explaining how asexual and sexual reproduction differ in their impact on potential mutation of offspring, i.e., describing which type of reproduction has a greater risk of mutation and why the risk is greater*) • the impact of heredity on organisms (traits, diseases, genetic disorders) (*e.g., describing how a trait such as body type can affect the lives of the members of a family across generations*) The student makes no major errors or omissions.
Score 2.5	No major errors or omissions regarding the score 2.0 elements and partial knowledge of the score 3.0 elements.
Score 2.0	**No major errors or omissions regarding the simpler details and processes such as:** • recognizing and recalling specific terminology, such as: egg, sperm, genetic mutation, offspring, organism, reproduction, heritable characteristics • recognizing and recalling isolated details, such as: – half the genes come from each parent in sexual reproduction – heritable characteristics determine an organism's likelihood to survive and reproduce **However, the student exhibits major errors or omissions with score 3.0 elements.**
Score 1.5	Partial knowledge of the score 2.0 elements but major errors or omissions regarding the score 3.0 elements.
Score 1.0	**With help, a partial understanding of some of the score 2.0 elements and some of the score 3.0 elements.**
Score 0.5	With help, a partial understanding of some of the score 2.0 but not the score 3.0 elements.
Score 0.0	**Even with help, no understanding or skill demonstrated.**

Table 3.3 depicts the measurement topic of biological diversity and evolution of life at the eighth grade. Similar scales would be designed for each measurement topic in grades kindergarten through grade 8 and for courses at the high school level. Use of scales like that in table 3.3 allows teachers to design and score their own assessments, with the added advantage that scores on those assessments are comparable from teacher to teacher. To illustrate, one teacher might design an assessment for the information in table 3.3 that employs a traditional format with multiple-choice items and short constructed-

response items. A second teacher might employ an assessment that is more project-based. Regardless of the differences in format, a score of 2.5 (let's say) on the two assessments would be interpreted in the same fashion—students demonstrated understanding of the simpler information (that is, the Score 2.0 content in table 3.3) and partial understanding of the more complex information (the Score 3.0 content in table 3.3).

Monitoring Phase 1

During Phase 1, district emphasis is on the development of reporting topics. There are at least two conventions that should be monitored. First, the number of reporting topics must be kept small. Reexamining the sample reporting topics in table 3.1, we see that there are less than twenty topics per subject area. Ideally, we recommend about fifteen topics per grade level per subject area.

Second, all reporting topics at each grade level should follow the basic rubric format depicted in table 3.2 and should follow a logical progression from grade level to grade level. To illustrate, consider table 3.4 from Marzano and Haystead (2008). It reports the Score 3.0 values for grades K–8 for the topic of number sense and number systems.

Table 3.4 Vertical Alignment of Content Across Grades K–8 for a Single Reporting Topic

Number Sense and Number Systems	
Grade 8	
Score 3.0	While engaged in grade-appropriate tasks, the student demonstrates an understanding of numbers and number systems by: • determining the union and intersection of various sets (*e.g., explaining and exemplifying the union of two sets as the set of elements that are in either set*) • using scientific notation to express large numbers and small numbers between 0 and 1 (*e.g., 0.256 written in scientific notation is 2.56 x 10^{-1}*) • distinguishing between subsets of the real number system (*e.g., explaining and exemplifying that a rational number is one that can be written as a simple fraction and providing examples of rational versus irrational numbers*) **The student exhibits no major errors or omissions.**
Grade 7	
Score 3.0	While engaged in grade-appropriate tasks, the student demonstrates an understanding of numbers and number systems by: • expressing various large numbers in multiple ways (*e.g., explaining and exemplifying how the same number can be expressed in scientific and standard notations*) • expressing various numbers in exponential form (*e.g., explaining and exemplifying the meaning of exponents that are negative or 0*) • comparing and ordering a variety of integers, fractions, decimals, and percents (*e.g., converting between different types of rational numbers for accurate comparison*) **The student exhibits no major errors or omissions.**

Grade 6	
	While engaged in grade-appropriate tasks, the student demonstrates an understanding of numbers and number systems by:
Score 3.0	• expressing various small numbers in multiple ways (*e.g., explaining and exemplifying how factors and exponents can be used to decompose and recompose whole numbers*)
	• using prime factorization (*e.g., explaining and exemplifying how prime factorization was used to solve a given problem*)
	• expressing decimal numbers in multiple ways (*e.g., explaining and exemplifying how a decimal number can be used to express the concepts of ratio, proportion, and percent*)
	The student exhibits no major errors or omissions.
Grade 5	
	While engaged in grade-appropriate tasks, the student demonstrates an understanding of numbers and number systems by:
Score 3.0	• expressing equivalent forms of various simple fractions (*e.g., explaining and exemplifying how to convert between simple fractions, decimals, and percents*)
	• rounding decimals to a given place value and fractions (*including mixed numbers*) to the nearest half (*e.g., explaining and exemplifying the rules for rounding a variety of numbers*)
	• finding the greatest common factor (GCF) and least common multiple (LCM) of a variety of numbers (*e.g., explaining and exemplifying the concepts of common multiples and factors*)
	The student exhibits no major errors or omissions.
Grade 4	
	While engaged in grade-appropriate tasks, the student demonstrates an understanding of numbers and number systems by:
Score 3.0	• ordering and comparing whole numbers (millions), decimals (thousandths), and fractions with like denominators (*e.g., converting between whole numbers, decimals, and fractions for accurate comparison*)
	• expressing complex money amounts in a variety of ways (*e.g., explaining and exemplifying how the same amount of money can be expressed differently*)
	• finding factors and multiples of whole numbers through 100 (*e.g., explaining and exemplifying the difference between a factor and a multiple*)
	The student exhibits no major errors or omissions.
Grade 3	
	While engaged in grade-appropriate tasks, the student demonstrates an understanding of numbers and number systems by:
Score 3.0	• using mathematical language and symbols to compare and order whole numbers (up to 9999), decimals (hundredths), and commonly used fractions and mixed numbers (*e.g., explaining and exemplifying the difference between < and ≤*)
	• generating equivalent forms of whole numbers (*e.g., explaining and exemplifying how different forms of a whole number are the same*)
	The student exhibits no major errors or omissions.

continued on next page ▶

Grade 2	
Score 3.0	**While engaged in grade-appropriate tasks, the student demonstrates an understanding of numbers and number systems by:** • using place value concepts to represent, compare, and order whole numbers (up to 999) (*e.g., explaining and exemplifying how each place represents a power of ten*) • representing different forms of money (*e.g., explaining and exemplifying how common decimal numbers, .10, .25, .50, and .75, are related to money*) **The student exhibits no major errors or omissions.**
Grade 1	
Score 3.0	**While engaged in grade-appropriate tasks, the student demonstrates an understanding of numbers and number systems by:** • generating equivalent forms for the same number (*e.g., explaining the difference between two equivalent forms of the same number*) • describing the value of a small collection of coins (total value up to one dollar) (*e.g., explaining the difference in value between different coins*) • describing and using ordinal numbers (first to tenth) (*e.g., explaining the position of different ordinal numbers*) **The student exhibits no major errors or omissions.**
Grade K	
Score 3.0	**While engaged in grade-appropriate tasks, the student demonstrates an understanding of numbers and number systems by:** • comparing and ordering whole numbers up to 10 (*e.g., explaining the quantity represented by different whole numbers*) • placing simple sets of objects into ordinal position (*e.g., explaining why one set of objects belongs in a specific ordinal position*) • constructing multiple sets of objects each containing the same number of objects (*e.g., making and describing equal sets out of a group of different objects*) **The student exhibits no major errors or omissions.**

Source: From *Making Standards Useful in the Classroom* (pp. 117–120), by Robert J. Marzano and Mark W. Haystead. Alexandria, VA: ASCD. © 2008 by ASCD. Used with permission. Learn more about ASCD at www.ascd.org.

Table 3.4 illustrates the recommended level of vertical alignment from grade level to grade level (and from course to course at the high school level). The reporting topic depicted in table 3.4 is number sense and number systems within the mathematics strand of numbers and operations. Typically, the expectation for a given grade level or course is found in the Score 3.0 elements. At eighth grade, students are expected to determine and explain the intersection of various sets. This involves explaining and exemplifying the union of two sets as the set of elements that are in either set. At the seventh-grade level, students are expected to express large numbers in multiple ways. This involves demonstrating how the same number can be expressed in scientific notation and in standard notation. At the sixth-grade level, students are expected to express various small numbers in multiple ways. At this grade level, the emphasis is on factors and exponents. At each successive grade level, then, a given reporting topic should address the same general category of knowledge as was addressed at the previous grade level, albeit with more advanced applications.

Phase 2: Track Student Progress on Measurement Topics Using Teacher-Designed and District-Designed Formative Assessment

During Phase 2, teachers are keeping track of student progress on selected measurement topics identified as areas of student need in specific schools and at specific grade levels. For example, one mathematics reporting topic might be identified for third-grade classes in one school, while a different mathematics topic is identified for the third-grade class in another school. Teachers in each school would keep track of students' progress on their respective topics using formative assessments.

With measurement topics articulated in scale format as depicted in table 3.3, teachers should have fairly strong guidance regarding how to design and score formative assessments for identified topics. Specifically, the scale or rubric designed by the district should be easily translated into formative assessments. To illustrate, consider the scale for the biological diversity of life in table 3.3. To design a formative assessment, the teacher would use the guidance provided in that figure and design Score 2.0, 3.0, and 4.0 items. Using the scale depicted in table 3.3, a teacher might design the formative assessment shown in table 3.5 (page 40).

Note that there are three sections to table 3.5: section A, section B, and section C. Section A includes Score 2.0 items, section B includes Score 3.0 items, and section C includes a Score 3.0 item. Each item in each section is designed to assess a specific component of knowledge from the scale shown in table 3.3.

Throughout a unit of instruction or a grading period, teachers would design assessments such as that depicted in table 3.5 as needed. Although different teachers would be using different assessments, the scores on those assessments would be comparable. Regardless of the assessment used, a score of 2.0 would indicate that students understand the simpler details and processes in the scale, but not the more complex information and processes (Score 3.0 knowledge); a score of 2.5 would indicate that students understand the simpler details and processes and received partial credit on the more complex information and processes and so on.

Table 3.5 Sample Formative Assessment for Biological Diversity of Life

Section A	
Match each term with one answer that best describes it.	
Vocabulary Term	*Answer*
• Egg	a. The process that results in an offspring that is an exact copy of the one parent.
• Sperm	b. An individual living system.
• Genetic mutation	c. A trait that can be passed from parents to offspring. d. The contribution of the female in the reproductive process.
• Offspring	e. Changes to the nucleotide sequence of the genetic material of an organism. f. The element of a cell that carries a single unit of information.
• Organism	g. The product of reproduction. h. The element of a cell that allows the cell to split.
• Reproduction	i. The contribution of the male in the reproductive process. j. The part of the cell that houses the chromosomes.
• Heritable characteristic	k. The biological process by which new individual organisms are produced.

Circle "T" if the statement is true and "F" if the statement is false.

T	F	Half the genes come from each parent in sexual reproduction.
T	F	Heritable characteristics determine an organism's likelihood to survive and reproduce.
T	F	Asexual reproduction involves two parents.
T	F	Bears reproduce asexually.

Section B

1. Write a short explanation of the differences between asexual and sexual reproduction in terms of the following:
    a. Risk of mutation
    b. Energy requirements
    c. Similarity of offspring to parent
    d. Processes involved
2. Select one of the following and explain how it affects a chosen organism.
    a. Inherited trait
    b. Disease
    c. Genetic disorder

Section C

1. Explain how a genetic disorder can be passed from parents to offspring when the parents are healthy.

In addition to formative assessment designed by individual classroom teachers, the district should construct formative assessments to be used by all teachers at a specific grade level for a specific reporting topic. This practice has been referred to as "common assessments" (Ainsworth & Viegut, 2006). While this is a useful endeavor, Marzano and Haystead (2008) also recommend a "common item bank" in addition to common assessments. To implement a data bank of common items, a district would generate Score 4.0, Score 3.0, and Score 2.0 items for each measurement topic at each grade level for K–8, and for each course at the high school level. Teachers could then use the items in the item bank to design their own unique assessments composed of common items.

Since formative assessments are designed to provide a view of students' learning over time, Phase 2 ultimately involves charting students' progress. To do so, teachers would provide students with a blank chart for each reporting topic like that in figure 3.2.

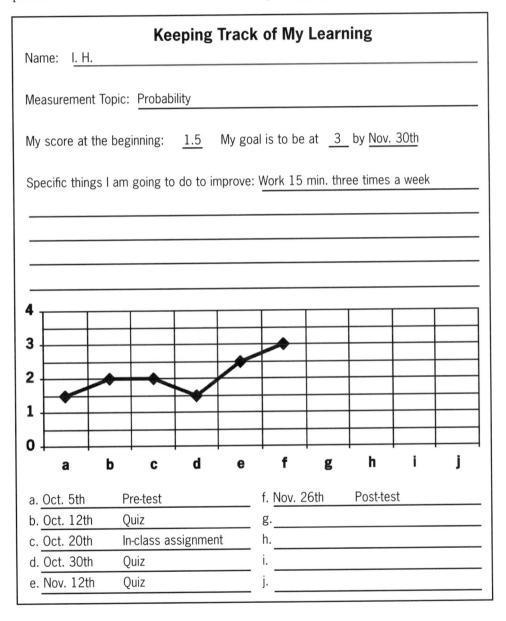

Figure 3.2 A sample student progress chart

The first column in figure 3.2 represents a formative assessment given by the teacher on October 5; this student received a score of 1.5 on that assessment. The second column represents the assessment on October 12; this student received a score of 2.0 on that assessment (and so on). Having each student keep track of his or her scores in this fashion provides them with a visual tracking of their progress. It also allows for powerful discussions between teacher and students. The teacher can discuss progress with each student regarding each reporting topic. Also, in a tracking system like this, the student and teacher are better able to communicate with parents regarding the student's progress in specific areas of information and skill.

One of the most powerful aspects of formative assessment is that it allows students to see their progress over time. In a formatively based system, virtually every student will "succeed" in the sense that every student will increase his or her knowledge relative to specific reporting topics. One student might have started with a score of 2.0 on a specific topic and then increased to a score of 3.5; another student might have started with a 1.0 and increased to a 2.5—both have learned and have exhibited about the same growth relative to the topic.

Knowledge gain is relatively easy to compute in a formatively based system. Again, consider figure 3.2. During this particular period of time, the student began with a score of 1.5 and ended up with a score of 3.0—a gain of 1.5 scale points. As we shall see in the discussion of Phase 4, this increase can be represented in report cards. *Knowledge gain,* then, is the currency of student success in a formatively based, value-added system.

Monitoring Phase 2

Monitoring Phase 2 involves ensuring that every teacher in the district is collecting formative assessment data on their students in a manner that allows for the identification of knowledge gain at the individual student level. This data should then be aggregated up to the classroom level, the school level, and the district level. Data at each level should be reviewed periodically. For example, once per month, a teacher might review the progress of his or her students on a specific measurement topic. Teachers would confer with each student comparing their initial status with their current status. A report would also be generated at the school level. Once per month, the principal in a school would generate a report like that in table 3.6 (page 43).

Table 3.6 Teacher-by-Teacher Report on Specific Mathematics, Reading, and Writing Topics at Grade 4

	Math Topic #1	Math Topic #2	Reading Topic #1	Reading Topic #2	Writing Topic #1	Writing Topic #2
Average gain						
Teacher #1	.56	.71	.62	.23	.41	.32
Teacher #2	.77	.65	.24	.31	.65	.42
Teacher #3	.68	.72	.35	.45	.35	.45
All grade 4 teachers	.67	.69	.40	.33	.47	.30

Table 3.6 reports the average knowledge gain for each of three fourth-grade teachers in a school for two mathematics topics, two reading topics, and two writing topics. Average gains for the school are also reported. Note that individual teacher identities are not disclosed. In this way, teachers can compare the performance of their students with that of others in an anonymous manner. Additionally, the school as a whole can examine the variability in performance from class to class or grade level to grade level. Similar reports would be generated comparing schools within the district.

Phase 3: Provide Support for Individual Students

The ultimate purpose of setting and monitoring achievement goals is to identify those students who are underperforming in terms of expected gain. The system of record keeping created in Phase 2 facilitates the identification of such students. For example, a district might set a nonnegotiable goal that every student must progress at least .5 scale points each quarter for specific topics in reading, writing, and mathematics. Some form of extra support would be made available to underperforming students (in terms of expected gain). There are a number of general approaches to extra support that a district might adopt. One obvious approach is to ensure high-quality instruction in every classroom. We address this in the next chapter. Here, we consider efforts outside regular classroom instruction.

The No Child Left Behind (NCLB) Act of 2001 focused attention on the potential use of outside school time (OST) programs. Such programs have existed for many years in the form of after school and summer school activities. As described by Lauer, Akiba, Wilkerson, Apthorp, Snow, and Martin-Glenn (2006), NCLB specifies that OST services "must occur outside the school day and be backed by evidence that the services are effective in raising student achievement" (p. 275). Lauer et al. further note that OST "does not imply a specific time, schedule, or duration, but it does mean that during those hours, children are doing something other than activities mandated by school attendance" (p. 276). In their analysis of the experimental research on OST programs for students considered "at risk," Lauer and colleagues identified some interesting patterns of findings. These patterns are summarized in table 3.7 (page 44).

Table 3.7 Research Findings Reported by Lauer et al. (2006) Regarding OST Programs

After School and Summer School		Average ES*d*	N of ES*d*	P gain
After School	Reading	.07	15	3
	Mathematics	.16	9	6
Summer School	Reading	.05	14	2
	Mathematics	.09	12	4
Grade Level		Average ES*d*	N of ES*d*	P gain
Lower Elementary (K–2)	Reading	.22	14	9
	Mathematics	NS	–	
Upper Elementary (3–5)	Reading	NS	–	
	Mathematics	.05	11	2
Grade Level (continued)		Average ES*d*	N of ES*d*	P gain
Middle School (6–8)	Reading	.09	9	4
	Mathematics	.16	11	6
High School (9–12)	Reading	.25	2	10
	Mathematics	.44	5	17
Focus		Average ES*d*	N of ES*d*	P Gain
Academic	Reading	.07	21	3
	Mathematics	.07	17	3
Academic and Social	Reading	NS		
	Mathematics	.19	5	8
Duration				
Reading	43 Hours or Less	NS		
	44–84 Hours	.28	7	11
	85–210 Hours	.15	8	6
	Greater Than 210 Hours	NS	–	
Mathematics	45 Hours or Less	NS		
	46–75 Hours	.23	4	9
	76–100 Hours	.22	4	9
	Greater Than 100 Hours	.16	3	6

Grouping				
		Average ESd	N of ESd	P gain
Large Groups (11 or More)	Reading	NS		
	Mathematics	.08	5	3
Small Groups (10 or Fewer)	Reading	NS		
	Mathematics	.18	3	7
One-to-One Tutoring	Reading	.50	5	19
	Mathematics	NS	–	
Mixed	Reading	.15	8	6
	Mathematics	.25	6	10

Note: Average ESd = average effect sizes; N of ESd = number of effect sizes; P gain = point gain.

Table 3.7 reports results as effect sizes (ESd; see Technical Note 3.1, page 138, for a discussion of ESd). Briefly, an ESd reports the expected gain (or loss) in standard deviation units associated with a particular variable. In this case, that variable is OST programs. To illustrate, consider the first row in table 3.7. The average effect size for after-school programs is .07. This average is based on 15 effect sizes (N of ESd) found by Lauer et al. (2006) in their meta-analysis. It means that reading achievement is increased by .07 standard deviations by after school OST programs. This translates into a 3 percentile point gain (P gain) in reading achievement.

If one accepts the findings in table 3.7 at face value, a number of inferences might be made. First, both after-school and summer school programs have a small to moderate impact on reading and mathematics achievement. Second, OST programs seem to have the greatest effect at the high school level. While the findings reported in table 3.7 are promising, they are not terribly strong in that one might expect more than a 3 percentile gain in reading and a 6 percentile gain in mathematics.

A second and more optimistic view of the effects of OST programs is provided by Durlak and Weissberg (2007). They examined sixty-six after-school programs that were designed to promote personal and social skills. They found results much more optimistic than those reported by Lauer et al. (2006) when they limited their investigation to thirty-nine programs that used "evidence-based" training strategies. Durlak and Weissberg define *evidence-based* training strategies as *sequenced* and *active*. Relative to sequencing, Durlak and Weissberg note,

> New skills cannot be acquired immediately. It takes time and effort to develop new behaviors and often more complicated skills must be broken down into smaller steps and sequentially mastered. Therefore, a coordinated sequence of activities is required that links the learning steps and provides youth with opportunities to connect these steps.

> Usually, this occurs through lesson plans or program manuals, particularly if programs use or adapt established criteria. (p. 10)

About active forms of learning, they note,

> Active forms of learning require youth to act on the material. That is, after youth receive some basic instruction they should then have the opportunity to practice new behaviors and receive feedback on their performance. This is accomplished through role playing and other types of behavioral rehearsal strategies, and the cycle of practice and feedback continues until mastery is achieved. These hands-on forms of learning are much preferred over exclusively didactic instruction, which rarely translates into behavioral change. (p. 10)

Durlak and Weissberg (2007) examined the effects of the thirty-nine evidence-based programs on three categories of outcomes: (1) feelings and attitudes, (2) behavioral adjustments, and (3) school performance. Feelings and attitudes involved two components: (1) students' self-perceptions and (2) school bonding. Effect sizes for these components were .35 and .26, respectively. Behavioral adjustments involved positive social behaviors, problem-solving behaviors, and cessation of drug use. Effect sizes for these outcomes were .30, .26, and .22, respectively. Of most interest to the discussion in this book are the findings for school performance that involved performance on academic achievement tests, grades, and school attendance. The results for these outcomes are reported in table 3.8.

Table 3.8 Results of Durlak and Weissberg (2007) Meta-Analysis on School Outcomes

	Average ESd	N of ESd	P gain
Academic Achievement Tests	.31	10	12
Grades	.24	9	10
School Attendance	Not significant ($p < .05$)	9	

Note: ESd = effect sizes; N of ESd = number of effect sizes; P gain = point gain.

Durlak and Weissberg report that to produce an effect on academic learning, OST programs have to have an "academic component" that involves either one-to-one tutoring or some form of help on homework. Table 3.8 illustrates that such efforts produce discernable effects regarding performance on achievement tests and grades.

Speaking of their findings for performance on academic tests, Durlak and Weissberg note,

> These particular results merit comment for two reasons: (1) the obtained mean effect of 0.31 is nearly twice as large as the effects found in the only other meta-analysis of ASPs [After School Programs] that has

reported significant changes on test scores (Lauer et al., 2006) and (2) the association between academic performance and personal and social development is of great interest to educators, researchers, and policy-makers. (p. 18)

To put the effect sizes reported by Lauer et al. (2006) and Durlak and Weissberg (2007) in perspective, consider the conclusions of experts on meta-analysis. Cooper, Charlton, Valentine, and Muhlenbruck (2000) note that an effect size of .10 or even lower should not be considered trivial. Similarly, Cohen (1988) has demonstrated that seemingly small effect sizes might be considered important when one examines them from the perspective of success versus failure on a specific assessment. To illustrate, consider the modest effect size of .07 for after-school reading programs reported by Lauer et al. (2006). The studies used to compute this effect size were performed on students at risk. Using Cohen's method of interpretation, one could infer that if 50% of these students could pass a specific test without the benefit of after-school programs, 53% would be able to pass after being involved in after-school programs. This is not a trivial increase for students at risk. Using the .31 effect size reported by Durlak and Weissberg (2007), one would predict that if 50% of students could pass a specific test without the benefit of after-school programs, 62% would pass after being involved in after-school programs, an even more dramatic increase in achievement (see Technical Note 3.2, page 139, for a discussion of how these figures were computed).

Monitoring Phase 3

Monitoring Phase 3 involves ensuring that all students who are underperforming in terms of expected knowledge gain are receiving some form of OST. These students would be identified using the data generated in Phase 2. Students who could not participate in OST programs would be offered some alternative such as one-to-one tutoring.

Given that identified students are properly placed in OST programs, the district would monitor their progress. Again, this would be accomplished using knowledge gain scores that would be closely monitored. To illustrate, consider table 3.9 (page 48), which reports gain scores for a particular student on particular reporting topics.

Table 3.9 depicts the gains for a single student during one quarter for six of twelve reporting topics. The remaining reporting topics were not addressed during this interval but would be addressed during other intervals. The student has exhibited a gain of .5 score points on two topics, a gain of 1.0 score points on three topics, and a gain of 1.5 score points on one topic. The report also identifies the student's status on the six topics at the conclusion of the quarter. Using this information, a student's progress and status on specific reporting topics can be monitored and appropriate interventions taken when necessary.

Table 3.9 Gain Score Graph for One Student

Reporting Topic	Gain for 1st Quarter	Final Status
1. Number sense and number systems	.5	1.5
2. Operations and estimation	.5	2.0
3. Addition and subtraction	1.0	2.0
4. Multiplication and division	1.0	3.0
5. Patterns, relations, and functions		
6. Algebraic reps and models		
7. Lines, angles, and geometric objects		
8. Transformations, congruency, and similarity		
9. Measurement systems		
10. Perimeter, area, and volume		
11. Data analysis and interpretation	1.5	2.5
12. Probability	1.0	2.0

Phase 4: Redesign Report Card

Reaching Phase 3 is indeed a noteworthy accomplishment. Student learning is being tracked on specific reporting topics, and those students in need of help outside of the regular classroom are receiving it. However, if the changes made at Phase 3 are to be maintained, a vehicle must be in place that institutionalizes tracking student programs, identifying students in need of help, and then providing that help. We believe that one of the most powerful ways to institutionalize such behavior is to use report cards like that shown in figure 3.3 (pages 49–51).

Figure 3.3 provides a sample report card for fifth grade, but it easily generalizes down to kindergarten and up to twelfth grade. For the purposes of this discussion, we will assume that the school using this report card is departmentalized for each subject. That is, different teachers are responsible for each subject area (as opposed to self-contained classrooms where one teacher addresses all subject areas). For this grading period, five subject areas have been addressed as follows: (1) language arts, (2) mathematics, (3) science, (4) social studies, and (5) art. Within each subject area, final topic scores are provided. Each teacher computed final topic scores using formative assessments. These topic scores are reported as bar graphs within each subject area. The student in figure 3.3 received a final score of 3.5 for the topic of word recognition and vocabulary in language arts; he received a final topic score of 2.5 for estimation in mathematics, a final topic score of 1.5 for matter and energy in science, and so on. Note that the bottom part of each bar is darker than the top part of each bar. The darker part of each bar represents where the student started at the beginning of the grading period. The lighter part of the bar represents knowledge gain during the grading period. For example, the

Name:	John Mark											
Address:	123 Some Street											
City:	Anytown, CO 80000											
Grade Level:	4											
Homeroom:	Ms. Smith											
Language Arts	2.46	C		Participation		3.40	A					
Mathematics	2.50	B		Work Completion		2.90	B					
Science	2.20	C		Behavior		3.40	A					
Social Studies	3.10	A		Working in Groups		2.70	B					
Art	3.00	A										
Language Arts												
Reading:												
Word Recognition and Vocabulary	2.5											
Reading for Main Idea	1.5											
Literary Analysis	2.0											
Writing:												
Language Conventions	3.5											
Organization and Focus	2.5											
Research and Technology	1.0											
Evaluation and Revision	2.5											
Writing Applications	3.0											
Listening and Speaking:												
Comprehension	3.0											
Organization and Delivery	3.0											
Analysis and Evaluation of Oral Media	2.5											
Speaking Applications	2.5											
Life Skills:												
Participation	4.0											
Work Completion	3.5											
Behavior	3.5											
Working in Groups	3.0											
Average for Language Arts	2.46											

Figure 3.3 Sample report card

continued on next page ▶

Mathematics		
Number Systems	3.5	
Estimation	3.0	
Addition/Subtraction	2.5	
Multiplication/Division	2.5	
Ratio/Proportion/Percent	1.0	
Life Skills:		
Participation	4.0	
Work Completion	2.0	
Behavior	3.5	
Working in Groups	2.0	
Average for Mathematics	2.50	
Science		
Matter and Energy	2.0	
Forces of Nature	2.5	
Diversity of Life	1.5	
Human Identity	3.5	
Interdependence of Life	1.5	
Life Skills:		
Participation	3.0	
Work Completion	1.5	
Behavior	2.5	
Working in Groups	1.0	
Average for Science	2.20	
Social Studies		
The Influence of Culture	3.5	
Current Events	3.0	
Personal Responsibility	4.0	
Government Representation	3.5	
Human and Civil Rights	1.5	
Life Skills:		
Participation	3.5	
Work Completion	3.5	

Behavior	3.5									
Working in Groups	4.0									
Average for Social Studies	3.10									
Art										
Purposes of Art	3.5									
Art Skills	3.0									
Art and Culture	2.5									
Life Skills:										
Participation	2.5									
Work Completion	4.0									
Behavior	4.0									
Working in Groups	3.5									
Average for Art	3.00									

student in figure 3.3 received a final score of 2.5 in word recognition and vocabulary. However, the student began the grading period at a score of 1.0. He exhibited a gain of 1.5 points on the scale. Contrast this with his score on literary analysis. He received a score of 2.0 at the end of the grading period. However, because the entire bar is in the darker shade, the student exhibited no growth throughout the grading period. He started at a score of 2.0 and ended at a 2.0. This lack of gain would signal a need for some type of intervention. Also note that each subject area has included academic and life-skill topics. Specifically, for each subject area, final topic scores and knowledge gain were computed for the life-skill topics of participation, work completion, behavior, and working in groups.

At the top of the report card, traditional A, B, and C letter grades are reported for each subject area (see Marzano, 2006, for a discussion of how rubric scores are translated to letter grades). In effect, then, the top part of the report card is quite traditional. However, the detail provided by the topic scores for each subject area is not. Topic scores provide students and parents with a quick and easily interpreted view of performance on all topics from which the grade was computed.

A report card like this could be accompanied by a traditional transcript that lists courses taken, credits earned (in the case of secondary schools), and an overall grade point average (GPA). While this system is not ideal, it does have two advantages. First, it provides a link to what people are familiar with in that it reports overall grades and a traditional GPA. Second, it reports the final scores for all topics addressed within a grading period along with the knowledge gain during that period. This provides far more information than traditional report cards. In addition, it provides a glimpse as to what a more useful and valid report card might be like.

There are many other types of report cards that might be used including those that separate out academic content from life skills and those that report no overall grades at all. For a discussion of these, see Marzano (2006) and Marzano and Haystead (2008).

Monitoring Phase 4

At Phase 4, the entire system of setting and monitoring goals for achievement should be in place, and all aspects of the system can be monitored, including the integrity and viability of measurement topics, teachers' use of formative assessments, identification of students at risk, and monitoring their enhanced achievement as a result of interventions. In addition, the new system of report cards should be monitored for integrity. Assigning grades has long been the prerogative of individual teachers. In this new system, teachers are not at liberty to construct their own methods of grading. Rather, the system should be the same among teachers responsible for the same course or subject area at a specific grade level.

Summary

This chapter addressed setting and monitoring nonnegotiable goals for achievement. The case was made that the most effective system would employ a value-added, formatively based approach to assessment as opposed to a status-oriented, summatively based approach. Four phases a district might progress through when designing such a system were identified. During Phase 1, state standards are reconstituted as reporting topics. Each reporting topic at each grade level is articulated in the form of a rubric or scale that can be used to design and score formative assessments. During Phase 2, student progress on specific topics is tracked using teacher-designed and district-designed formative assessments. During Phase 3, students who are not exhibiting adequate knowledge growth are identified and extra support for these students is provided by the district. During Phase 4, report cards are changed so that they reflect student status and knowledge gain in each reporting topic.

4 Setting and Monitoring Nonnegotiable Goals for Instruction

Setting and monitoring nonnegotiable goals for instruction at the district level might not be as obvious a need as is setting and monitoring nonnegotiable goals for achievement (see chapter 3). However, recall the findings reported in chapter 2 from the OECD study of the highest-performing school systems in the world. All ten systems focused on ensuring effective teachers in every classroom. It was their singular method of enhancing student achievement.

A singular focus on instruction is quite consistent with the NCLB mandate of 2002. Specifically, in the 2002 report *Meeting the Highly Qualified Teachers Challenge* (U.S. Department of Education), then Secretary of Education Rod Paige noted,

> Just a few months ago, President George W. Bush and the United States Congress issued a compelling challenge to our nation: to ensure that in this great land, no child is left behind. . . . As part of the *No Child Left Behind Act*, Congress issued another challenge to ensure that, by the end of the 2005-2006 school year, every classroom in America has a teacher who is "highly qualified." After all, only with a talented teacher in every classroom will our students have the opportunity to excel. Will our nation meet the "highly qualified teachers" challenge? As this report explains, this challenge will be met only if our state policies on teacher preparation and certification change dramatically. (p. iii)

Even a brief examination of the research on the influence of effective teachers demonstrates why this is a logical aspect of NCLB and a wise step to take at the district level. Specifically, a growing number of studies have quantified the effect a teacher can have on student achievement (for discussions, see Haycock, 1998; Marzano, 2003; Nye, Konstantopoulos, & Hedges, 2004). To illustrate, the study by Nye et al. (2004) involved random assignment of students to classes and controlled for factors such as previous achievement of students, socioeconomic status, ethnicity, gender, and class size. Nye and colleagues summarize the results as follows:

> These findings would suggest that the difference in achievement gains between having a 25th percentile teacher (a not so effective teacher) and a 75th percentile teacher (an effective teacher) is over one-third of a standard deviation (0.35) in reading and almost half a standard deviation (0.48) in mathematics. Similarly, the difference in achievement gains between having a 50th percentile teacher (an average teacher) and a 90th percentile teacher (a very effective teacher) is about one-third of a standard deviation (0.33) in reading and somewhat smaller than half a standard deviation (0.46) in mathematics. . . . These effects are certainly large enough effects to have policy significance. (p. 253)

It is important to note that the Nye et al. (2004) study was conducted in lower elementary grades. However, given the statistical controls they employed and the existence of similar findings at higher grade levels, one can reasonably conclude that a focus on high-quality teaching at the district level is a wise endeavor.

Characteristics of High-Quality Teachers

To understand the district-level responsibility of setting and monitoring nonnegotiable goals for instruction, it is necessary to understand the characteristics of high-quality teachers. One frequently cited characteristic is experience, and one frequently cited study on the importance of teacher experience is that by Ferguson (1991). Linda Darling-Hammond (1997) describes the study in the following way:

> In an analysis of 900 Texas school districts Ronald Ferguson found that teachers' experiences—as measured by scores on a licensing examination, master's degrees, and experience—accounted for about 40% of the measured variance in students' reading and mathematics achievement at grades 1 through 11, more than any other single factor. (p. 8)

Another characteristic often cited regarding teacher effectiveness is certification or licensure (Armour-Thomas, Clay, Domanico, Bruno, & Allen, 1989). For example, licensure is one of the three critical factors mentioned in a landmark report entitled *What Matters Most: Teaching for America's Future* (National Commission on Teaching and America's Future, 1998). The report used the metaphor of a "three-legged stool" for quality assurance:

> The three-legged stool of quality assurance—teacher education program accreditation, initial teacher licensing, and advanced professional certification—is becoming more sturdy as a continuum of standards has been developed to guide teacher learning across the career. (p. 29)

Subject-matter knowledge is another apparent feature of high-quality teachers (Andrews, Blackmon, & Mackey, 1980; Haney, Madaus, & Kreitzer, 1987; Schalock, 1979; Soar, Medley, & Coker, 1983). It is one of the primary variables identified in *What Matters Most*. Unfortunately, Hill (2007) reports a rather disturbing finding regarding teacher subject-matter knowledge among middle school mathematics teachers. Specifically, she notes that teachers with the most mathematical knowledge and experience tend not to be working with those students with the greatest needs.

The relationship between subject-matter knowledge and effective teaching, however, is not straightforward. That is, one cannot say that those with the most subject-matter knowledge are necessarily the best teachers. Reviews of the research commonly reveal an uneven relationship between teacher subject-matter knowledge and student achievement. Byrne (1983) reviewed thirty-one studies and found that only seven showed a positive relationship between teacher subject-matter knowledge and student achievement. Ashton and Crocker (1987) reviewed fourteen studies and reported that only five found positive relationships between teacher subject-matter knowledge and student achievement. Monk (1994) reported that a threshold level of subject-matter knowledge is necessary for effective teaching, but after a certain point, such knowledge does not have a strong relationship with student achievement. Taken together, these findings imply that a critical level of subject-matter knowledge is needed for effective teaching, but beyond that point, the relationship between teacher subject-matter knowledge and student achievement begins to taper off. Additionally, it is reasonable to assume that the critical level of knowledge is different from grade level to grade level. The critical level of subject-matter knowledge required to teach third-grade mathematics is certainly far less than the critical level of subject-matter knowledge required to teach tenth-grade mathematics.

The discussion thus far points to a fairly straightforward approach to a district-level emphasis on effective teaching in every classroom—recruit the most highly qualified teachers and retain them. We certainly believe that this should be a top priority of every district. However, effective recruitment and retainment might not be the only road to ensuring high-quality instruction. Rather, fostering high levels of pedagogical knowledge can also dramatically enhance the quality of teaching in a district. As Darling-Hammond (2000) notes:

> It may be that the positive effects of subject matter are augmented or offset by knowledge of how to teach the subject to various students. That is, the degree of pedagogical skill may interact with subject-matter knowledge to bolster or reduce teacher performance. (p. 6)

In a study of 200 teachers, Ferguson and Womack (1993) reported that the amount of pedagogical courses teachers took accounted for four times the variance in teacher performance than did subject-matter knowledge. In a study involving some 7,500 eighth-grade students, Weglinsky (2000) reported that participation in professional development activities accounted for significant amounts of variance in mathematics and science achievement. Specifically, teacher experience and involvement in professional development activities accounted for about as much variance in student achievement as did student background. In a study of the relative effects of teacher background qualification, attitudes, and instructional practices, Palardy and Rumberger (2008) concluded,

> The results indicate that compared with instructional practices, background qualifications have less robust associations with achievement gains. These findings suggest that the No Child Left Behind Act's "highly qualified teacher" provision, which screens teachers on the basis of their background qualifications, is insufficient for ensuring that classrooms are led by teachers who are effective in raising student achievement. To meet that objective, educational policy needs to be directed toward improving aspects of teaching, such as instructional practices and teacher attitudes. (p. 111)

Similar sentiments about the importance of pedagogical knowledge have been echoed by many other researchers (Brown, Smith, & Stein, 1995; Byrne, 1983; Wiley & Yoon, 1995).

A Focus on Pedagogy

Taken as a whole, the preceding discussion highlights the importance of recruiting and retaining teachers who are experienced, have proven track records of enhancing student achievement, and are well grounded in subject-matter content. However, this is not the only action a district can and should take. In addition to effective hiring and retainment practices, our findings suggest that districts should have an explicit goal regarding the continuous improvement of pedagogical skills among teachers in the district. Such a goal is consistent with the apparent purpose of professional learning communities (PLCs). As described by Stoll, Bolam, McMahon, Wallace, and Thomas (2006), the label *professional learning community* is used in a wide variety of ways. However, most discussions of PLCs emphasize the importance of teachers enhancing their pedagogical skills in a reflective, cooperative manner:

> There appears to be broad international consensus that it [a PLC] suggests a group of people sharing and critically interrogating their practice in an ongoing, reflective, collaborative, inclusive, learning-oriented, growth-promoting way (Mitchell & Sackney, 2000; Toole & Louis, 2002); operating as a collective enterprise (King & Newmann, 2001). (Stoll et al., 2006, p. 223)

While recruiting and retaining high-quality teachers is a practice a district can begin immediately, enhancing the pedagogical skills of teachers probably occurs over time. We believe it takes a considerable amount of time to develop a district in which enhancement of pedagogical skills occurs systematically and comprehensively. Building on the suggestions of Marzano (2007c, 2008), we have identified five phases to developing such a system.

Phase 1: Systematically Explore and Examine Instructional Strategies

Over the years, various models of effective pedagogy have been proposed (such as Hunter, 1984). While a case can be made that a district should simply adopt one of these models, a case can also be made that "off the shelf" interventions are short-lived in K–12 education. This point was made by Cuban (1987), who chronicled the fate of a number of interventions, all of which were basically sound and had supporting research. Some of the more visible ones that have not endured are programmed instruction, open education, the platoon system, and flexible scheduling. A viable option to adopting an instructional model is to develop a district-specific approach through action research. Reeves (2008) asserts that use of action research is one of the most powerful manifestations of teacher leadership.

Nolen and Putten (2007) explain that action research was first introduced as a research methodology in the 1950s "in response to the growing need for more relevant and practical knowledge in the social sciences: It bridged the gap between academic research and day-to-day applications" (p. 401). Chiseri-Strater and Sunstein (2006) describe action research conducted by teachers in terms of praxis. They note that praxis involves "connecting our ideas with our actions, deriving theories from our practices. . . . [It] gives us the power to understand teaching as a kind of scholarship and resists ideas that confuse our common sense. We reclaim internal agency for ourselves as inquisitive, successful professionals when we take the time to ask what works and then try to answer it" (p. xxii).

Action research, for the purposes discussed here, begins with the identification of specific instructional techniques that are to be studied. This typically means selecting strategies from an existing list of effective practices. For example, relative to instructional strategies, Marzano, Pickering, and Pollock (2001) identified the following nine instructional strategies as supported by research:

1. Identifying similarities and differences

2. Summarizing and note taking

3. Reinforcing effort and providing recognition

4. Homework and practice

5. Nonlinguistic representations

6. Cooperative learning

7. Setting objectives and providing feedback

8. Generating and testing hypotheses

9. Questions, cues, and advance organizers

Relative to classroom management strategies, Marzano, Pickering, and Marzano (2003) identified the following four areas:

1. Rules and procedures

2. Disciplinary interventions

3. Teacher–student relationships

4. Teacher mental set

Other similar lists of effective strategies have been developed by Good and Brophy (2003) and Mayer (2003).

Once a reference list of instruction and management strategies has been identified, teachers throughout the district can conduct action research projects on a voluntary basis. Teacher action research can be quite informal or formal. At an informal level, teachers might simply try strategies in their classrooms and then record their impressions of how well the strategies worked. Reeves (2008), for example, reviews case studies conducted by teachers at various grade levels and attests to their impact on student achievement and teacher professional behavior.

At a more formal and more rigorous level, teachers can design and carry out studies involving experimental classes (classes in which a specific strategy is employed) and control classes (classes in which the selected strategy is not employed). In our experience, these types of projects are the most powerful tools in developing a model of instruction since they establish a more credible causal link between use of an instructional strategy and student achievement. Table 4.1 (page 59) summarizes data from 113 experimental/control action research studies conducted in ten different schools (see Marzano & Associates, 2005; www.marzanoresearch.com).

The results in table 4.1 are reported in terms of effect sizes as opposed to correlations. As described in chapter 3 and Technical Note 3.1 (page 138), an effect size reports the difference between the mean in the experimental group and control group in standard deviation form. For example, an effect size of .39 means that the average score in the experimental group is .39 standard deviations greater than the average score in the control group. This would be associated with a 15 percentile point gain in achievement.

Table 4.1 Distribution of 113 Effect Sizes (ES*d*) From Action Research Projects

Mean ES*d*	.39
Median ES*d*	.28
Range	6.67
10th percentile	−.43
20th percentile	−.17
25th percentile	−.06
30th percentile	.06
40th percentile	.15
50th percentile	.28
60th percentile	.33
70th percentile	.61
75th percentile	.70
80th percentile	.90
90th percentile	1.44

One interesting aspect of the findings reported in table 4.1 is that they were produced with minimal professional development. The 113 teachers who participated in the experimental/control studies had a modicum of staff development for the instructional strategies they employed. For example, the vast majority of teachers participated in a one-day or half-day professional development workshop regarding the use of specific instructional strategies, read a brief description of the instructional strategies, or both. Given that Prentice and Miller (1992) contend that effect sizes must be judged not simply on their magnitude but also on the resources they require, even a moderate average effect size of .39 as reported in table 4.1 is considerable.

Monitoring Phase 1

Monitoring Phase 1 involves keeping track of teacher participation in action research projects. While action research should not be mandated, it should be considered the norm in a district. As part of their professionalism and professional development, all teachers should be expected to engage in public and private inquiries into the effectiveness of their instruction. Reeves (2008) provides a variety of ways this can be fostered. We recommend that districts and schools encourage and provide the necessary incentives and resources for teachers to conduct action research studies in their classrooms. As much as possible, these studies should be experimental/control in nature. To this end, the district should provide support in analyzing and interpreting the findings in a way that maximizes the generalizability of the conclusion. (For examples of how findings might be reported for public consumption, see Marzano & Associates, 2005.) In effect, we recommend that districts engage in long-term and continuous examination of the impact of specific instructional and management strategies used by their teachers.

This work should result in a growing database from which decisions about common instructional and management practices can emanate.

The end goal of Phase 1 is to build a district culture that embraces collective and continuous inquiry regarding effective pedagogy. This is an aspect of what Goddard, Hoy, and Hoy (2004) refer to as "collective efficacy." According to Goddard et al. (2004), the collective efficacy of the teachers in a school is a better predictor of student success in schools than the socioeconomic status of students. In simple terms, collective efficacy is the shared belief that "we can make a difference." Arguably, one of the most powerful ways that this belief can be fostered is to collect data like that demonstrated in table 4.1. Teachers will have direct evidence to their collective efficacy when they see that use of specific strategies directly affects student achievement in a positive way.

While Phase 1 is continuous in the sense that districts should continually be adding to their database of action research studies regarding specific instructional and management techniques, it typically takes from one to two semesters for a district to amass enough action research projects to move on to Phase 2.

Phase 2: Design a Model or Language of Instruction

Once a critical mass of action research studies have been conducted around specific instructional strategies, a district is in a position to design a model or "language of instruction." An instructional model should not be misconstrued as an attempt to constrain teachers to one particular approach to teaching: it should be interpreted as a necessary vehicle for communication between teachers regarding the art and science of teaching. A common language or model as a tool for effective communication is addressed implicitly and explicitly by those who promote the importance of PLCs (Stoll et al., 2006; Hord, 2004; King & Newmann, 2001).

One issue that should be considered when developing a model or language of instruction is how general or specific it will be. History would suggest that it should not be too narrow in focus. Recall Madeline Hunter's lesson design. It contained seven "steps": (1) anticipatory set, (2) objective and purpose, (3) input, (4) modeling, (5) checking for understanding, (6) guided practice, and (7) independent practice (Hunter, 1984). While it was highly useful, Hunter's lesson design was perhaps too focused on a single lesson and did not take into account the context in which lessons occur. That is, a lesson occurs in the context of a unit. The demands of a unit at a given point in time surely change the dynamics of a given lesson. Consequently, one lesson within a unit might be focused on teaching a new skill. In that case, Hunter's lesson design makes perfect sense. Another lesson within the same unit might focus on students' working on long-term projects. In that case, Hunter's lesson design is not as useful.

As an alternative, Marzano (2007b) has developed a set of "design questions" that are meant to be applied to unit design as opposed to lesson design. They are depicted in table 4.2.

Table 4.2 Instructional Design Questions

1. What will I do to establish and communicate learning goals, track student progress, and celebrate success?
2. What will I do to help students effectively interact with new knowledge?
3. What will I do to help students practice and deepen their understanding of new knowledge?
4. What will I do to help students generate and test hypotheses about new knowledge?
5. What will I do to engage students?
6. What will I do to establish or maintain classroom rules and procedures?
7. What will I do to recognize and acknowledge adherence and lack of adherence to classroom rules and procedures?
8. What will I do to establish and maintain effective relationships with students?
9. What will I do to communicate high expectations for all students?
10. What will I do to develop effective lessons organized into a cohesive unit?

An instructional model based on design questions such as these has an advantage over a model that focuses on lessons. It allows a great deal of flexibility in terms of how teachers approach pedagogy while at the same time providing specific guidance in that endeavor.

Monitoring Phase 2

Monitoring Phase 2 should focus on the specificity and flexibility of the instructional model designed by the district. The model should be specific enough to provide guidance for teachers, but flexible enough to allow for different teaching styles. To this end, we recommend the question format depicted in table 4.2, which focuses on unit design as opposed to lesson design. This allows for teacher creativity in the day-to-day work of the classroom. We also recommend that districts produce a written document describing their model. Some districts with whom we have worked have generated their own manuals and provided in-service training in these models for new and veteran teachers. Finally, we recommend that individual schools within a district be allowed to adapt the model to their specific needs and circumstances. This might involve adding components or altering components of the district model. In this way, individual schools will have a personal investment in the model used in their school.

Phase 3: Have Teachers Systematically Interact About the Model or Language of Instruction

A model of instruction is powerful only if used as a vehicle for communication—as the basis for conversations about effective teaching. Louis, Kruse, and Associates (1995) refer to such conversations as reflective dialogue. Little (2002) emphasizes the importance of naturally occurring interactions among teachers regarding instruction. While naturally occurring interactions should be encouraged, structured conversations should also be designed.

Dimmock (2000) notes that providing teachers with the time and space to interact about instruction is critical to promoting professional dialogue among teachers; however, time and space are not sufficient. A format and structure for such interactions should be developed. To illustrate, one district with whom we have worked uses "late starts" on a monthly basis. During late starts, teachers meet in small grade-level or subject-matter teams to discuss instructional issues. Between late-start meetings, teachers are asked to record their reactions to instructional techniques from the district model they had tried. The record keeping for teachers is kept to a minimum. Teachers spend a few minutes after a particular class in which they have tried a strategy recording comments like those depicted in table 4.3.

Table 4.3 Teacher Reactions to Specific Strategies

Focus area:
I'm going to work on the part of question 3 that deals with elaborating on what students have learned using comparison and contrast.
Reaction:
(Nov. 5) This took more time than I thought to get through the comparison activity. It also seemed harder than it should be.   (Nov. 7) I'm surprised that the kids remembered what we did 2 days ago about polynomials. This might have worked better than I thought.

Table 4.3 presents data collected from a teacher who has tried instructional strategies associated with Design Question 3 from table 4.2. At the end of a lesson in which a specific strategy had been tried, the teacher recorded his perceptions. On November 5, the teacher was not impressed with the effects of the strategy. Two days later, November 7, the teacher was beginning to see an effect on students.

During their late-start days, teachers discuss their recorded observations using the following protocol:

- Describe the strategy or strategies you tried.

- Describe its effect on student learning and the evidence for your conclusions.

- Describe areas for improvement on your part.

- Describe areas of strength on your part.

A variation on this approach has been suggested by DuFour and Marzano (2009). They note that in addition to teachers collecting data on the instructional strategies they have tried, they should also design common assessments using the scale depicted in table 3.2 (page 34). Teachers then bring their formative assessment scores and graphs of student progress to those meetings. In this way, teachers can discuss the effectiveness of the strategies they tried in the context of data from formative classroom assessments.

Monitoring Phase 3

Monitoring Phase 3 involves at least two components. First, schools should have a specific time each month (at least) during which teachers interact about instruction and examine the impact of their instruction on student achievement. This might vary from school to school based on their schedules and cultures. For example, one elementary school might employ late starts as the scheduled time when teachers interact about effective teaching using the model. Another elementary school might employ early dismissals. At the middle school level, extra time might be established during grade-level team meetings. At the high school level, extra time might be allotted during regularly scheduled departmental meetings. Regardless of the schedules they use, each school should have frequent (at least once per month) and systematic meetings where teachers share their experiences regarding their teaching experiments.

Second, district leadership should monitor the quality of interaction occurring between teachers. Stated differently, district leadership should have evidence that interactions among teachers focus on instructional practices. The time set aside for interacting about instruction should not be squandered on important but tangential issues such as administrative issues, general announcements, and socializing. To this end, brief notes might be taken at each meeting and summarized for each school. These school-level reports might be periodically reviewed at the district level.

Phase 4: Have Teachers Observe Master Teachers (and Each Other) Using the Model of Instruction

Teachers systematically talking about instruction will go a long way to creating a culture that is focused on teaching. However, nothing will put instruction in the spotlight as well as teachers observing other teachers. Louis et al. (1995) note that ultimately, professional learning communities must foster the "deprivatization of practice." This is perhaps one of the most difficult aspects of PLCs to implement. In his book *A Place Called School*, which summarized data from 1,350 elementary and secondary teachers, Goodlad (1984) noted that teachers generally report that they would like to observe others: "approximately three quarters of our sample at all levels of schooling indicted that they would like to observe other teachers at work" (p. 188). Flinders (1988) comments on the same phenomenon in his article "Teacher Isolation and the New Reform." Flinders explains that although teachers work in isolation, they seek professional interactions with colleagues. Similar observations have been made by Shulman (2004).

Here we recommend a very specific approach to teachers observing teachers. The approach operationally defines a *master teacher* as one who produces substantial gains in student learning. This is in contrast to defining a master teacher as one who uses specific instructional strategies. Although this might seem counterintuitive, it has a strong logic. Given the complexity of the teaching/learning process, it is safe to say that no model of instruction or set of instructional strategies could completely define effective teaching. Therefore, defining effective teaching as using specific instructional strategies is inherently myopic and dangerously misleading. This sentiment has been expressed directly or indirectly by many researchers and theorists (Willms, 1992; Reynolds & Teddlie, 2000; Berliner, 1986; Marzano, 2007c). Rather, different teachers employing the same instructional techniques might produce very different results in student learning. Consequently, overall effectiveness in teaching must be defined in terms of the one indisputable criterion for success—student learning.

Of course, to identify master teachers, a district must have a way to determine student learning in each teacher's class. The use of the scale and the measurement topics described in chapter 3 can be a great aid to this end. If measurement topics have been designed using the scale depicted in table 3.2 (page 34), then student learning can be compared from teacher to teacher—a score of 3.0 on one teacher's scale means the same thing as 3.0 on another teacher's scale. Additionally, a gain of 0.5 points for students in one class means about the same thing as a gain of 0.5 in another class. Master teachers would be operationally defined as teachers who consistently produce learning gains in their students.

Once master teachers have been identified, each master teacher's instructional strengths can be articulated using the district's model of instruction. To illustrate, assume that the ten design questions depicted in table 4.2 (page 61) have been adopted by a district. Within a particular school, a particular master teacher might be identified who demonstrates exceptional skill at Design Questions 1 and 3. Another master teacher might be identified who demonstrates exceptional skill at Questions 2 and 5, and so on. On a voluntary basis, teachers who wish to improve their instructional prowess would sign up to observe master teachers for specific design questions. For example, if a teacher wanted to observe an expert in Design Question 5—student engagement— he or she would seek out one of the district's master teachers who was particularly adept in this area. Ideally, the master teacher for Question 5 would also visit the classroom of the teacher seeking assistance to provide guidance and feedback to that teacher.

Monitoring Phase 4

One aspect of monitoring Phase 4 involves determining the extent to which master teachers have been identified and are available to all teachers. In an ideal world, every building in a district would have an adequate number of master teachers who are expert in a variety of aspects of the district's instructional model. However, this goal is probably not attainable. Consequently, provisions must be made for teachers seeking help to visit the classrooms of master teachers (in specific design questions) in buildings other than their own.

Another aspect of Phase 4 that should be monitored is the extent to which teachers in the district are taking advantage of the opportunity to observe master teachers. It seems reasonable that every teacher should request the opportunity to observe another teacher at least once every year or two.

Phase 5: Monitor the Effectiveness of Individual Teaching Styles

Once a clear model or language of instruction has been developed and a system of observation of master teachers has been implemented, then instruction can be monitored. One qualification should be made here. By *monitoring*, we do not mean that all teachers should be required to execute all aspects of the district's or school's instructional model. Recall that the model should be flexible enough to allow for differences in teaching style. Fullan (2001) explains that the purpose of teacher observation is to produce shared knowledge through interaction, which can be applied by teachers to solve real-world problems. Hord (1997) echoes these comments, noting that shared knowledge regarding instruction should translate into practical tools that can be used by teachers to enhance student achievement. The underlying sentiment in Fullan's and Hord's comments is that teachers must be allowed to have some flexibility in the way they approach instruction. It is certainly true that teachers should share a common language of instruction. It is also true that all teachers should have the common goal of enhanced student achievement. But in terms of the use of specific instructional techniques, the manner in which one teacher achieves this goal might be quite different from the manner in which another teacher accomplishes the same goal. Stated differently, teachers should be allowed to have different "profiles" regarding their use of specific instructional strategies. However, there should be no variation in expectations about student learning from teacher to teacher. All students should be expected to exhibit knowledge gain in every class.

Tucker and Strange (2005) recommend a very similar approach. They note that in the NCLB legislation, a *highly qualified teacher* is defined in terms of credentialing.

They explain that use of effective strategies and student knowledge gain should also be entered into the equation:

> According to the legislation, "highly qualified" teachers are defined as those who hold at least a bachelor's degree, are fully licensed or certified by the state in the subjects they teach, and can demonstrate competence in the subjects they teach.
>
> While licensure or certification is a significant indicator of teacher quality, these factors alone are insufficient for teacher effectiveness. [Teacher effectiveness] includes dispositions and an array of planning, organizational, instructional, and assessment skills . . . A "highly qualified" teacher is certainly a good starting point, but most of us would want our child to have a *highly effective* [emphasis added] teacher whose teaching effort yields high rates of student learning. (p. 6)

Later, Tucker and Stronge note that it is poor practice simply to focus on teachers' use of instructional strategies and make judgments regarding teacher effectiveness based on such observations. Rather, student knowledge gain should be the ultimate criterion for effective teaching:

> We don't suggest throwing out the use of classroom observation to foster teacher improvement; rather we advocate that teacher effectiveness be judged and demonstrated by both classroom instruction *and* [original emphasis] the learning gains of students. (p. 7)

To operationalize the suggestions of Tucker and Stronge, a district must collect teacher data and student data. For teachers, data would be collected on the extent to which they adhere to the elements of the district and school instructional model. Marzano (2008) recommends that rubrics be designed for each component of the instructional model. To illustrate, consider the rubric in table 4.4 (page 67). It is used to assess teacher skill at Design Question 1 from table 4.2 (page 61).

Using rubrics such as that depicted in table 4.4, a profile for each teacher can be compiled through teacher self-reports and observations by administrators. Regarding self-reports, teachers can rate themselves on a systematic basis and compile these ratings. Additionally, administrators can make systematic observations of teachers. These two sources of data can be combined to construct composite scores on various elements of the instructional model for each teacher. To illustrate, consider table 4.5 (page 68). The first eleven columns depict teacher self-report scores and supervisory scores for a group of teachers in a particular school.

Table 4.4 Teacher Rubric for Design Question 1: What Will I Do to Establish and Communicate Learning Goals, Track Student Progress, and Celebrate Success?

Score 4.0	In addition to Score 3.0 behaviors, adaptations that enhance students' learning.
Score 3.5	In addition to Score 3.0 behaviors, partial success with adaptations that enhance students' learning.
Score 3.0	While engaged in classroom activities that involve establishing and communicating learning goals, tracking student progress and celebrating success, the teacher makes no major errors or omissions regarding the following behaviors: • Presents students with a clearly defined scale or rubric for each learning goal • Allows students to identify their own learning goals in addition to those presented to them • Designs and administers formative assessments for each learning goal • Displays progress on learning goals for the whole class and facilitates students tracking their own progress • Recognizes individual student status and progress as well as that of the whole class
Score 2.5	No major errors or omissions regarding the simpler behaviors (Score 2.0 performance) and partial success at the more complex behaviors (Score 3.0 performance).
Score 2.0	No major errors or omissions regarding the following simpler behaviors: • Makes a distinction between learning goals and learning activities • Presents learning goals but does not design a scale for each • Designs and administers assessments for each learning goal but does not use a formative system • Tracks student progress but does not facilitate students tracking their own progress or does not display progress for the whole class • Recognizes and celebrates individual status and progress or group status and progress but not both However, the teacher exhibits major errors or omissions regarding the more complex behaviors (Score 3.0 performance).
Score 1.5	Partial success at the simpler behaviors (Score 2.0 performance) but major errors or omissions regarding the more complex behaviors (Score 3.0 performance).
Score 1.0	With help, partial success at some of the simpler behaviors (Score 2.0 performance) and some of the more complex behaviors (Score 3.0 performance).
Score 0.5	With help, partial success at some of the simpler behaviors (Score 2.0 performance) but not the more complex behaviors (Score 3.0 performance).
Score 0.0	Even with help, no success with the Score 2.0 or 3.0 behaviors.

Table 4.5 Teacher Self-Report Scores and Supervisor Scores

Teacher	Q1	Q2	Q3	Q4	Q5	Q6	Q7	Q8	Q9	Q10	Pre/post Gain	Engagement	Student Learning
Teacher 417	2.5	2.5	3.0	2.0	2.0	3.0	4.0	3.5	3.0	2.5	.76	2.11	3.09
Supervisor			2.5			3.0			2.5				
Teacher B13	2.0	3.0	2.5	3.0	3.5	2.5	3.0	2.0	2.5	3.0	1.33	3.23	3.06
Supervisor		2.0			2.5	2.5							
School Average	2.34	2.46	3.01	2.77	3.11	2.67	2.84	2.91	3.01	3.12	.53	2.33	2.56
District Average	2.67	2.87	2.84	3.01	2.78	2.41	2.86	2.73	3.08	3.04	.47	2.77	2.41

Source: *Getting Serious About School Reform* (Marzano, 2008). Used with permission.

As shown in table 4.5, teacher self-report scores on all ten design questions have been collected. In a given year, a teacher should be able to rate herself on each of the ten questions. However, supervisor scores are not reported for all ten design questions. This is because a supervisor would not have the time to make valid observations on all ten questions in a single year. Consequently, in a given year, a supervisor—in consultation with a given teacher—would identify a few design questions to observe. Over the years, scores on all design questions for each teacher could be attained from supervisors.

To complete the profile for each teacher, student data must also be collected. Student data are reported in the last three columns of table 4.5. We recommend at least three types of student data. The first is pre-test/post-test data from a specific unit of instruction. This is shown in the column of table 4.5 labeled *pre/post gain*. These pre-test/post-test scores should all use the same metric. If the scale depicted in table 3.2 (page 34) is used, this metric will be a 0 through 4.0 scale with half-point scores. The pre-tests and post-tests can either be teacher-made assessments or common assessments designed by the district. As described in chapter 3, use of the common scale shown in table 3.2 renders scores from teacher to teacher more comparable.

Another type of data that should be collected is student self-report data. Two obvious areas for student self-report data are student learning and student engagement. The last two columns in table 4.5 report this type of data. The *engagement* column contains average scores on a four-point Likert-type survey item regarding the extent to which students rate their level of engagement during instruction. This item would be answered anonymously by students. The last column in table 4.5 (*student learning*) contains average scores from a four-point Likert-type survey item regarding the extent to which students believe they have learned new content during instruction. This item also would be answered anonymously by students.

This type of data would be collected once per semester during a specific interval of time (for example, during a specific unit of instruction for a given teacher). Note that each teacher has an identification (ID) code (such as teacher 417, teacher B13) known only to the teacher and administrators. The first ten columns after the teacher ID code represent teacher and supervisor ratings on the ten design questions of the instructional model. The next column reports the average pre-test/post-test gain for students. The last two columns report the average engagement and learning scores from the self-report survey items. The last two rows in the report contain the average for all teachers in a building and the average for all teachers in the district.

It is certainly not the case that every teacher should be expected to meet or exceed the district or school average on all measures. Again, each teacher is unique in his or her instructional profile. However, comparison between individual teacher profiles and school and district averages should be the basis for discussions between teachers and supervisors. More specifically, individual teachers would identify specific goals for improvement with their supervisor. The focal point of such deliberation should always be student learning and engagement. An individual teacher might set a goal of raising the pre-test/post-test achievement gain from .5 to .6 and raising the average level of student engagement by one half a scale point by the end of the year. The teacher might also elect to focus on one specific instructional design question to achieve these goals. For example, after examining his or her instructional profile as compared with the profiles of others in the district, a teacher might select Design Question 1 of the district's model on which to focus during the year. That selection might be made because the teacher notes that his or her scores on that design question are significantly lower than the school or district averages. The teacher and administrator contrast the findings with the specific goals that were set when data are collected the second semester.

Monitoring Phase 5

Monitoring Phase 5 involves ensuring that data are collected on teachers and students in a systematic and uniform manner. We recommend that data are collected twice each school year. Individual teacher data at each school should be collected at the district level to ensure fidelity to data collection procedures. The extent to which specific goals are set for each teacher regarding student learning as well as goals for increased expertise in specific aspects of the instructional model should also be monitored at the district level. It is reasonable to expect that the number of master teachers (defined by student learning) in the district would gradually increase from year to year. Finally, the district should monitor the extent to which student learning is increasing. This can be done by examining the learning gains in individual classrooms throughout the span of a year. It should also be done by examining scores on state-level tests and tests designed within the district.

Summary

This chapter addressed setting and monitoring nonnegotiable goals for instruction. A case was made that this goal can and should be addressed by recruiting and retaining highly qualified teachers. However, this goal should also be addressed by developing a system designed to continuously improve the pedagogical skills of teachers. Five phases to this end were identified. During Phase 1, teachers systematically explore and examine instructional strategies using action research. During Phase 2, the district designs a model or language of instruction that allows for individual schools to make their own adaptations. During Phase 3, teachers systematically interact about the model. Time must be provided by the district for these interactions to occur. During Phase 4, teachers observe master teachers using the model of instruction. Master teachers are not defined as those who use all aspects of the instructional model; rather, they are defined as teachers who consistently produce knowledge gain in their students. During Phase 5, the district monitors the effectiveness of individual teaching styles by correlating teachers' skills at using the strategies in the instructional model with student engagement and learning.

5 Collaborative Goal Setting, Board Alignment, and Allocation of Resources

This chapter addresses three related findings from our study: (1) collaborative goal setting, (2) board alignment with nonnegotiable goals for achievement and instruction, and (3) allocation of resources to support nonnegotiable goals. While setting and monitoring nonnegotiable goals for achievement and instruction are certainly the centerpiece of the type of changes necessary for districts to approach high-reliability status, the three factors addressed in this chapter are necessary conditions for these goals to be met. *Collaborative goal setting* is the vehicle used to establish nonnegotiable goals for achievement and instruction; *board alignment* is necessary to sustain long-term attention to these goals; and *resources* must be *allocated* to fund activities such as professional development, scheduling changes, and the like. Recall that in chapter 3, we represented the relationship between collaborative goal setting, board alignment, allocation of resources, and nonnegotiable goals for achievement and instruction as depicted in figure 5.1 (page 72).

Figure 5.1 indicates that collaborative goal setting, board alignment, and allocation of resources are the foundation on which nonnegotiable goals for achievement and instruction can be reached. Collaborative goal setting is the starting place for setting these nonnegotiable goals. Once goals are established, they must be supported by board alignment and adequate resources must be allocated to them. Given its place in this series of events, we begin with collaborative goal setting.

Collaborative Goal Setting

The need for a collaborative goal-setting process has been highlighted by researchers and theorists for at least four decades. For example, Goodlad (1995) and Frieri (1970) have long called for a collaborative goal-setting process involving all significant

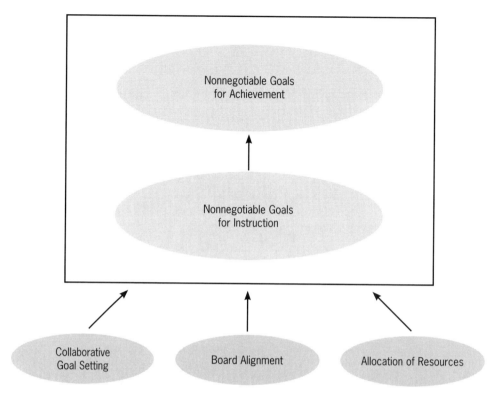

Figure 5.1 Relationship between collaborative goal setting, board alignment, allocation of resources, and nonnegotiable goals for achievement and instruction

stakeholders. Recent years have seen a number of organizations explicitly acknowledging the need for a goal-setting process that involves a broad array of constituents. In 2002, the Connecticut State Board of Education (CSBE) issued a position statement on educational leadership in which they emphasized the importance of a district adopting a collaborative approach to improving student achievement:

> District leaders must establish and support effective leadership structures that include all members of the school district team. The new leadership paradigm must move districts and schools toward becoming a collaborative learning community, focused on student learning. (2002, p. 1)

They further noted that a collaborative team should include but not be limited to the superintendent, school board members, principals, teachers, students, and members of the community. Without the involvement of these groups in an atmosphere of creative problem solving regarding the singular goal of enhancing student achievement, little of substance can be accomplished.

Ward (2007) echoes the importance of engaging all important stakeholders in serious reform issues: "The time is right for board members, superintendents, and principals to engage other leaders at all levels of the organization. It's the smart thing to do—and it's the right thing to do" (p. 20). However, he also provides the following caution:

> While practitioners and others with a stake in improving schools should help solve big picture challenges, board members and administrators should be careful in deciding whom to engage in the process and how to engage them. You must consider first whether prospective participants are ready, willing and able to play a role. (p. 27)

Ward's caution is significant. Just because disparate groups assemble does not mean that all are dedicated to a common goal of enhancing student achievement. By inference, one can assume that consensus must be established regarding the purpose of collaborating before engaging in the process of collaborative goal setting. Lest this caution imply that collaborative goal setting is impossible, Hardy (2007) cites a number of examples of successful efforts including the following:

- In Canton, Ohio, the mayor and the school board meet on a regular basis, and the city and schools have launched a joint effort to renovate and rebuild 19 schools.

- In Fort Worth, Texas, the school board and the city council have a regular dialogue, and they have formed a joint security initiative in the schools.

- In Las Vegas, city council members lunch regularly with principals and administrators to discuss school and neighborhood issues.

- In Orlando, city and school officials have established the Parramore Kidz Zone (modeled after the Harlem Kids Project), which provides extra services to children in this low-income community. (p. 39)

In a study of eleven school districts that had successfully negotiated large-scale systemic reform, Green and Etheridge (2005) note that a key factor to the success of these systems was identifying and recruiting leaders who sought collaborative input:

> It was clear that new leadership did not reside solely with central administration; rather leadership was collaborative and shared across the district among individuals who were able to facilitate attainment of the vision and mission. They set the tone for whether or not collaboration occurred or continued. In fact, these new leaders were sought, hired, or elected because of their inclusive leadership style. They exhibited particular traits that facilitated participatory governance of the district and fostered collaborative working relationships among district employees, union members, and citizens. (p. 824)

One constituent group that must be included in any collaborative goal-setting effort but is consistently singled out as a possible source of problems is teacher unions. Unfortunately, in some places, the relationship between teacher unions, superintendents, and school boards is not amenable to collaborative goal setting. Witness the following titles of articles regarding the strain in relationships between teacher unions and other groups within a school district reported by Wynn (1983, reported in Sell, 2006):

Tricks Unions Like to Play on School Boards

How to Handle a School Board Spy

Get Tough: Give Teachers a Dose of Their Own Medicine

Step Up the Crossfire: File More Grievances

Getting a Pound of Flesh

About the perceptions of teacher unions, Sell (2006) notes that although they certainly have the right to demand for adequate resources and working conditions, teacher unions sometimes have a disproportionate and negative influence on the running of a district. Commenting on the excessive influence of teacher unions, Fantini (1975) notes, "They can determine when a teacher will work, and often with what children. They determine how many children will be in a classroom. They determine how many times a year a principal will supervise a teacher, what type of program will be offered, etc." (p. 2).

Plecki, McCleery, and Knapp (2006) contend that critics of teacher unions commonly complain that they put the good of their membership above the good of students. Moreover, teacher unions are the most influential group in school board elections and are the least satisfied of all interest groups. Sell (2006) explains that school boards are commonly caught in a bind when interacting with rigid teacher unions during negations. School boards are accountable to the community, state, and federal government and view decisions about the district from a broad perspective, whereas teacher unions might view decisions about the district from the perspective of the ease or difficulty of the teachers' work-life only.

Relationships between teacher unions and school boards are not the only challenges to a collaborative goal-setting process. School boards have not always related well with school superintendents. As Sell notes, "As long as superintendents and school boards have worked together, the question has existed: who actually has the authority to run schools?" (p. 79) Superintendents can be put in a compromising position with school boards, given that the latter is the official governing agency in a district and has the power to retain or dismiss a superintendent. Such a relationship can create a dynamic in which the superintendent is more focused on pleasing his or her employer (that is, the school board) than enhancing the achievement of students. This dynamic is particularly evident in the relationship between the superintendent and the school board president.

Board Alignment and Support

Once goals for achievement and instruction have been established through a collaborative goal-setting process, board alignment and support for the goals must be firmly established. School boards have been inextricably linked to the fate of districts from the beginning of formal schooling in the United States. To understand the role of school boards in the dynamics of district reform, it is useful to briefly review their history. Glass, Bjork, and Brunner (2000) provide a panoramic perspective of that history. We draw from their accounts.

School boards can be traced to town meetings established in Massachusetts in the late 1700s. The position of the school superintendent was established in the 1830s. Up until that point, unpaid and part-time board members managed schools, but geometrically growing school populations forced school boards to hire full-time personnel. By the 1860s, twenty-seven cities had full-time superintendents. This represented a major shift of power from the group (the school board) to the individual (the superintendent). Some school boards gave up power willingly; others did not.

In the early part of the twentieth century, many superintendents took on the role of proselytizing for the common school along with fighting against political spoils systems that frequently determined which textbooks would be purchased, which vendors would be used to provide school service, and which teachers and principals would be hired. This period was followed by a movement toward a more scientific approach to management following the principles of Frederick Taylor. By the 1930s, the movement had evolved to an emphasis on hiring specialists to help run districts. Where the superintendent was responsible for the overall well-being of the district; subject-matter specialists, who focused on only one subject (mathematics, science, and so on), were hired along with non–subject matter specialists such as school psychologists and school nurses.

Throughout the first part of the twentieth century, school boards moved gradually to the practice of meeting periodically for the purpose of setting policy. The day-to-day running of the district was left up to the superintendent. Over time, hierarchical lines of authority became more clearly defined.

In the 1950s, school boards were populated by prominent professional people in a community such as local chamber of commerce members, doctors, and lawyers. Many of these people came to the position believing their job was to represent the overall interests of the community. Beginning in the 1960s, the constitution of school boards shifted to blue-collar workers, home makers, and citizens who had specific agendas regarding changes that should be made in the district. Ever since school boards have been selected through a popular vote, the representativeness of that vote has been an issue. For example, Plecki et al. (2006) note that "recent research has found that only 10 percent to 15 percent of the electorate, on average across the nation, votes in school board elections" (p. 17).

The 1960s and 1970s were also characterized by criticisms from school reformers. Particularly loud criticisms were heard from parents of minority students who perceived schools as not only unresponsive to the needs of minority students but also, in some cases, wittingly or unwittingly working against the achievement of minority students. Given their high visibility, superintendents became prime targets for school reformers, and the firing of high-profile superintendents made front page news. As noted by Glass et al. (2000), "The tension that existed in society during this tumultuous time spilled over to the schools and led to a superintendency much different from the one that existed during the quiet years of the 1950s" (pp. 4–5).

The 1980s were characterized by calls for comprehensive reform of schools and districts. As Glass et al. (2000) note, "The 1980s will likely be remembered as the time in American public education when many players—the private corporate sector, politicians, and citizens of all races and socioeconomic levels—became sufficiently displeased to trigger a nationwide reform movement" (p. 5). This was due in no small part to the publication of *A Nation at Risk* (National Commission on Excellence in Education, 1983), which charged that the very security of the United States was threatened by the inadequacy of the K–12 public school system. This allegation sparked a school reform movement that placed great emphasis on state test scores. This, in turn, placed pressure on superintendents to become skilled at test interpretation and the use of test results to guide decisions regarding future district efforts. The focus for districts in the 1980s was accountability to the general public.

The 1990s saw a continued emphasis on accountability. The standards movement swept the country, making accountability even more specific in nature. Districts were expected to demonstrate high levels of achievement in specific subject areas at multiple grade levels. In effect, this forced district administrators to address specific elements of the curriculum, such as continuity of the curriculum from grades K–12 as it related to state standards and state tests. The net effect of the heightened emphasis on accountability was the creation of more bureaucracy to monitor test results and standards implementation. The 1990s also saw the rise of the "choice" movement. Many reformers made strong cases that competition was the best remedy for a system that had been otherwise impervious to change. Home schooling, charter schools, and vouchers gained significant ground during the 1990s.

Today the emphasis on accountability continues. As noted by the Institute for Educational Leadership (2001),

> In one form or another, all but a few states have new, tougher academic standards for all students, a radical change from the time when only 25 to 30 percent of students were expected to get the kind of high quality education that would allow them, for example, to go to college. Accompanying the new standards are more stringent **accountability** [original emphasis] rules, including incentives for students and schools

to improve and penalties if they do not. Many states now have "report cards" for districts and schools, not just for students, that are released annually with much fanfare. A district's rating on its report card can affect everything from the continued tenure of the superintendent to the market value of homes in the community. This represents a sea change for district leaders, since districts and schools were traditionally accountable for managing the educational process, not for getting specific academic results, which is, of course, a far more difficult assignment. (pp. 2–3)

The accountability movement has put school boards in a new, unfamiliar environment. Plecki et al. (2006) and others (Howell, 2005; Land, 2002; Conley, 2003) note that historically, schools boards have not focused on student achievement. Additionally, some believe that the accountability movement has decreased the traditional power of school boards. As Sell (2006) explains,

In the case of No Child Left Behind (NCLB), the reauthorization of the *Elementary and Secondary Education ACT* in 2002, districts were expected to implement reforms immediately or suffer the consequences of a loss of federal money or school restructuring. The question is not whether NCLB's directives are flawed, but whether it is wrong on a constitutional level to take power from the states and local boards when it comes to distributing funds. Of course, the funds in question are federal monies; however, given that jurisdiction over education is granted to the states, should the federal government be able to place such restrictive ties on education money? Regardless of the answer to this question, with each new legislative measure, more power is taken from local school boards' decision-making abilities. (pp. 76–78)

Allocation of Resources

Resources are the lifeblood of any reform effort. Much of the discussion and research regarding resources has focused on financial resources allocated to schools typically measured in per pupil expenditures (PPE). In a series of studies, Hanushek (1981, 1986, 1989, 1991) concluded that financial resources do not appear to have a strong and consistent relationship with student achievement. Hedges, Laine, and Greenwald (1994) reanalyzed many of the studies cited by Hanushek and reported different findings. They concluded that the relationship between financial resources and student achievement was positive and large enough to have implications for educational policy. In 1996, Greenwald, Hedges, and Laine (1996a) analyzed studies spanning three decades. Among many findings, they concluded that a $500 increase in per pupil expenditures is associated with an effect size (ES*d*) of .15 in terms of student achievement (see Technical Note 3.1, page 138, for a discussion of ES*d*):

> An increase in PPE of $500 would be associated with an increase in achievement of nearly a sixth of one standard deviation. This is a somewhat smaller effect than was estimated in our reanalysis (Hedges et al., 1994), but is derived from a more reliable, higher-quality and more recent data set. (p. 380)

To put this finding in perspective, consider a student at the 50th percentile in his or her overall achievement. If the district was to increase its per pupil expenditure by $500, one would predict the student's achievement to increase to about the 56th percentile based on the findings of Greenwald et al. (1996a); similarly, if the district was to increase its per pupil expenditure by $1,000, one would predict the student's achievement to increase to about the 62nd percentile. Greenwald et al. also computed estimates of the effect on student achievement of using a proportion of the $500 increase in specific ways. This is depicted in table 5.1.

Table 5.1 Effect on Student Achievement of Specific Uses of Expenditures

Specific Use of Additional $500 Expenditure per Student	ESd	Percentile Gain
Teacher salaries	.16	6
Teacher education[a]	.22	9
Retaining and hiring experienced teachers[b]	.18	7
Reducing teacher/pupil ratio[c]	.04	2

Note: Computed using data from Greenwald, Hedges, and Laine (1996a, p. 379).
   a. Teacher education addressed acquisition of a master's degree.
   b. Teacher experience addressed years of experience for teachers.
   c. Greenwald, Hedges, and Laine (1996a) caution that this might be an underestimate of the ESd for teacher/pupil ratio.

Table 5.1 indicates that when a portion of the increase of $500 in per pupil expenditures is funneled into teacher salaries, the expected result is an increase in student achievement of 6 percentile points (see Greenwald et al., 1996a, for details as to the exact percentage of the $500 that would be used for teacher salaries). The expected gain is 9 percentile points when those same dollars are funneled into teacher education. An increase in per pupil expenditures would result in a 7 percentile point gain when funneled into hiring and retaining more experienced teachers, and it would translate into a 2 percentile point gain when funneled into decreasing teacher/pupil ratio.

It is instructive to note that Hanushek (1996) challenged the conclusions of Greenwald, Hedges, and Laine, asserting that it is not money per se that has a positive relationship with student achievement, but the resources on which the money is spent.

He cites the findings from the Panel on the Economics of Education Reform that recommended a fundamental shift in the accountability of how schools use resources:

> Concern about the continuing misallocation of education resources led the Panel on the Economics of Education Reform (PEER) to call for fundamental changes in views about education policy. The PEER report, *Making Schools Work* (Hanushek, 1994), concludes that developing more effective schools is crucial to the future health of the U.S. economy. At the same time, the current structure of schools, with a lack of consequential performance incentives and with a tradition of not learning from the alternative approaches and programs that are tried, offers little reason unless there is a real change in focus. (Hanushek, 1996, p. 397)

In a response to Hanushek, Greenwald, Hedges, and Laine (1996b) noted the following:

> All of this necessitates an understanding of how money matters in education. However, before this is addressed the fact that so many children attend schools with limited resources demands that policymakers examine empirical evidence about the question of whether money matters. Our findings, which demonstrate that money, and the resources those dollars buy, do matter to the quality of a child's education [sic]. Thus policies must change to ensure that all children have sufficient resources *and* [original emphasis] that incentives to spend those resources wisely are in place. Even Hanushek now appears to concede this point. (p. 415)

In effect, although they do not agree as to the relative importance of increasing financial resources to schools, Hanushek and Greenwald, Hedges, and Laine appear to agree that financial resources are related to student achievement, and they agree that financial resources must be spent wisely. This appears to be the crux of the financial resource issue—how should money be spent? One useful lens with which to address this question is to compare how U.S. schools spend their money with those from other countries.

The United States Versus Other Countries

Comparisons between the United States and other countries are frequently made in terms of student achievement (see, for example, Stevenson & Stigler, 1992; Stigler & Hiebert, 1999). Commonly, Japan and Germany are used as reference points for discussions about the achievement of U.S. students. Based on data reported by Mullis et al. (1998) and Gonzales (2004), the following comparison can be made. When compared with other industrialized countries at the fourth grade, Japan ranks 3rd in mathematics and the United States ranks 8th (scores for Germany are not reported). At the eighth grade, Japan ranks 4th, whereas the United States ranks 12th (scores for Germany are not reported). At the tenth grade, Japan ranks 5th in mathematics literacy, Germany ranks 7th, and the United States ranks 26th. Finally, when general mathematics achievement is assessed in the final year of secondary school, Germany ranks 12th and the United States ranks 18th (scores for Japan are not recorded).

In science, the pattern is similar. At the fourth grade, Japan ranks 2nd and the United States ranks 5th (scores for Germany are not reported). At the eighth grade, Japan ranks 4th and the United States ranks 7th (scores for Germany are not reported). Finally, when general science knowledge is assessed in the final year of secondary school, Germany ranks 12th, whereas the United States ranks 16th (scores for Japan are not reported).

While comparisons between the United States and other countries have been challenged (see Baker & LeTendre, 2005), the consensus among educators and the general populous appears to be that the United States does not fare well in comparison with other countries when it comes to student achievement. Comparisons of resource allocations such as those depicted in table 5.2 provide an interesting perspective.

Table 5.2 Total Dollars Spent on Education and Total Dollars Spent on Students (Primary and Secondary)

	US Dollars Spent per Student	Percentage of GDP Equivalent
Germany	6,034	3.3
Japan	5,913	3.0
United States	7,877	3.9

Note: Percentage of GDP = Percentage of gross domestic product for total dollars spent for students
Data computed from Sen, Partelow, & Miller (2005, p. 17).

Table 5.2 indicates that the United States allocates more than Germany and Japan to per pupil expenditures. If one was to take the Greenwald et al. (1996a) study discussed previously at face value, one would expect the United States to outperform Germany and Japan since the United States outspends Germany and Japan on education. From the preceding discussion, it is clear that the United States does not outperform Germany and Japan in student achievement. However, recall from table 5.1 that it is not how *much* money is spent, but *how* money is spent that affects student achievement. Table 5.3 contrasts expenditures on teacher salaries for the United States, Japan, and Germany.

Table 5.3 Teacher Salaries in the United States, Japan, and Germany

	Salary in US Dollars for Experienced Teachers	Ratio to GDP	Salary in US Dollars for Novice Teachers	Ratio to GDP
Germany	52,839	1.99	43,100	1.62
Japan	43,069	1.63	22,800	.86
United States	41,708	1.19	28,806	.82

Note: Ratio to GDP = Ratio of average salary to gross domestic product (GDP) per capita.
Data computed from Sen, Partelow, & Miller (2005, p. 53).

Table 5.3 indicates that Germany and the United States have higher salaries for novice teachers than does Japan; however, both Germany and Japan outspend the United States when it comes to salaries for experienced teachers. This is noteworthy when interpreted in light of Greenwald et al.'s (1996a) finding that teacher experience has an effect size (ES*d*) of .18 and teacher education has an effect size of .22. These two factors have greater effect sizes than the more general indicator of per pupil expenditures. One might infer that higher salaries for experienced teachers would tend to keep more experienced teachers in a system. Similar conclusions might be reached regarding teacher education, which had the highest effect size reported by Greenwald et al. (1996a; see table 5.1).

Along with differences in teacher salaries, Japan, Germany, and the United States approach teacher preparation and professional development somewhat differently. Teachers in Japan must earn a certain number of credits in pedagogy or specialty subjects (more pedagogy for lower-level teaching and more specialty subject courses for upper levels). In addition, they must receive a teaching certificate. Within a school, administrators are careful to make sure that novice teachers have experienced mentors teaching at their grade level. Additionally, experienced teachers often informally provide assistance to novice teachers. Part of this spirit of cooperation might be because of scheduled collaborative interactions between teachers. For example, teachers have brief meetings every morning and share a common room for leisure and work activities (National Institute on Student Achievement, Curriculum, and Assessment; Office of Educational Research and Improvement; U.S. Department of Education, 1998). During their sixth, tenth, and twentieth years, advanced training is required of experienced teachers. In addition, many teachers apply for what amounts to teaching fellowships. Some of these fellowships might manifest as weekend workshops, and some might manifest as training in another country for approximately one month. These fellowship experiences are considered prestigious and are sought by many teachers.

In Germany, teachers train for six or seven years before taking over a classroom of their own (National Institute on Student Achievement, Curriculum, and Assessment; Office of Educational Research and Improvement; U.S. Department of Education, 1999). This includes university training and two years of student teaching. Student teachers have a mentor or a master teacher, although teachers are not uniformly accepting of this policy. A variety of ongoing continuing education classes are offered for teachers as they progress, but few states require teacher attendance. Teachers in the former West Germany are given civil-servant status after passing assessments based on in-class observations given during the first three years of teaching. Passing these tests means teachers cannot be fired. Teachers belong to unions, but because of their civil-servant status they cannot strike. Although they cannot be fired, teachers are evaluated every four to six years after receiving civil-servant status. These evaluations are mainly for promotional purposes although promotions are difficult to obtain. Even teachers who are not promoted receive raises based on number of years of service.

The United States appears to focus on the acquisition of degrees. Roughly 51% of U.S. teachers (primary and secondary) have a bachelor's degree as their highest degree, 41% have a master's degree, and 8% have a PhD. About 82.2% of teachers in the United States have four or more years experience, and roughly 18% are novice (three years or less) teachers. Approximately 77.4% of public schools require teachers to have full standard state certification. Remaining schools have varying levels of educational requirements. Ongoing teacher training is not nationally compulsory, but about 80% of public school districts and private schools offer systematic professional development regarding advances in curriculum, instruction, and assessment.

An interesting point of departure between U.S. teachers and those in other countries is the amount of time they actually teach. This is depicted in table 5.4.

Table 5.4 Teaching Time per Year in Hours

	Primary	Lower Secondary	Upper Secondary
Germany	784	735	684
Japan	635	557	478
United States	1,139	1,127	1,121

Note: Lower secondary can be roughly interpreted as middle school; upper secondary can be roughly interpreted as high school.
Data computed from Sen, Partelow, & Miller (2005, p. 55).

Taken at face value, table 5.4 indicates that U.S. teachers have very little time in school to engage in such necessary activities as planning for upcoming lessons, planning for units, correcting papers, developing new activities for students, examining their own effectiveness, and so on. This is because U.S. teachers spend more time teaching and, therefore, have less time in school to prepare. This could be a major block to any substantive reform in U.S. education in that most reforms of note take time to learn and adapt. Teachers might have little time to do anything but teach the students currently in their charge. At the same time, major reform movements are calling for increased time for teachers to study their craft and interact about effective instruction. Consider, for example, the recommendations of DuFour, Eaker, and DuFour (2005) regarding professional learning communities (PLCs). Among other recommendations, they call for teachers planning together, developing and scoring assessments together, reading and discussing professional literature together, and observing each other using instructional strategies. All of these require time outside of the classroom. All would appear to be impossible unless districts and schools lighten the teaching load for U.S. teachers.

In addition to the manner in which U.S. districts spend their resources on teachers, it is constructive to consider how resources are allocated to schools that have a majority of students in poverty as opposed to schools that do not. According to a 1997 report by the Council for Educational Development and Research, during a twenty-five-year period starting in 1969, the total number of persons living in poverty in the United States rose from 12.1% to 15.1% of the population. During this period, the percentage of persons older than sixty-five living in poverty decreased from 25.3% to 11.7 percent. The report notes, "The rise in child poverty is reflected in the schools; the number of poor children as a percentage of public school enrollment has grown from 14.4 percent in 1969–70 to 22.7 percent in 1994–1995" (p. 6).

The achievement differences for students who live in poverty versus those who do not are well documented. To illustrate, consider table 5.5. The pattern of achievement depicted in table 5.5 paints a compelling picture. The higher the percentage of students of poverty in a school, the lower the scores in mathematics and science. Apparently, this is not the case in other countries. Using TIMSS twelfth-grade mathematics data, Baker and LeTendre (2005) report patterns indicating that the United States does not do as well as other countries when it comes to educating its poorer students. This is depicted in table 5.6.

Table 5.5 Differences in Achievement by Percentage of Students of Poverty

	Less Than 10% Poverty Students	10% to 24.9% Poverty	25% to 49.9% Poverty	50% to 74.9% Poverty	75% or More Poverty Students	U.S. Average Score
Fourth grade mathematics	567	543	533	500	471	518
Fourth grade science	579	567	551	519	480	536
Eighth grade mathematics	547	531	505	480	444	504
Eighth grade science	571	554	529	504	461	527

Data computed from Mullis, Martin, Gonzalez, & Chrostowski (2004b, 2004c).

Table 5.6 Achievement for Students With Mothers Without a High School Degree

Students With Mothers Without a High School Degree (average proportion per nation = 29%)	Mean Math Achievement Score
Netherlands and Sweden	551–560
Denmark	541–550
Iceland and New Zealand	531–540
Austria, Norway, and Switzerland	521–530
France and Australia	511–520 (international average)
Canada	501–510
Germany	461–470
United States	441–450

Data computed from Baker & LeTendre (2005).

In table 5.6, poverty status is indicated by a mother's lack of completion of a high school degree. Again the pattern is clear. Among thirteen countries, the United States ranks last when it comes to the achievement of students of poverty.

To study the issue of educating children of poverty, Baker and LeTendre (2005) constructed what they refer to as a measure of inequality for basic educational resources:

> [The measure of inequality for basic educational resources included] budget for teaching materials, supplies, libraries, heating and lighting, and other physical plant resources; instructional space; computer hardware and software; professional experience of teachers; and student-to-teacher ratios (class size). We also restricted the analysis to middle grade schools in order to lessen the chance of including some intentional resource differences across curricular streams in upper secondary schools. (pp. 67–77)

One of the fundamental conclusions from their analysis was "wealthier nations tend to have less inequality in resources across schools, although there are a few interesting exceptions among them the United States" (p. 77). Baker and LeTendre (2005) further note that some nations, such as Japan, not only strive to equalize spending across socioeconomic status levels but also believe that those students with less resources at home should receive more resources at school. This might be thought of as policy guided by the motto "Equal is not always fair."

Baker and LeTendre caution that critics of U.S. education should not take their findings as evidence that U.S. schools are discriminating against students of poverty:

> Advocates for American disadvantaged children turn to almost paranoiac images of planned, sustained systematic racism and social classism in educational policy. Kozol's otherwise moving account of educational inequality in the United States is a classic example of this, suffering from an unrealistic image of an officially unstated yet systematic and oppressive educational policy presumably blessed by an uncaring American majority. (p. 80)

Of course, Baker and LeTendre are referring to Kozol's popular book *Savage Inequalities* (1992), which strongly implies a reasoned and systemic campaign in U.S. schools to underfund and underserve children of poverty. This notwithstanding, any consideration of resource allocations in U.S. education must come to grips with the simple fact that U.S. schools do not compensate for the lack of resources available to children of poverty. As Roza (2005) notes,

> Imagine an urban school district spending $2,900 more per pupil in one school than in another—generating an additional $900,000 for the school. One might speculate that the additional spending is driven

by student needs, but in this real life example, it has nothing at all to do with the kids. The reality is that spending varies significantly from school to school within a district. And while some spending variations among schools result from differing student needs, much more is driven by the antiquated, often haphazard, budgeting practices typical in large urban school districts. (p. 2)

Warner-King and Smith-Casem (2005) echo Roza's (2005) conclusions in their review of the research on resource allocation and students of poverty: "A growing body of research has uncovered evidence that schools serving high concentrations of poor, minority, and low-performing students receive fewer resources than other schools in the same district" (p. 1). They explain that many of these discrepancies are caused by budgeting practices in large districts that subdivide districts into subunits that sometimes use different funding categories and different allocation algorithms.

Summary

This chapter has addressed three findings: (1) collaborative goal setting, (2) board alignment with nonnegotiable goals for achievement and instruction, and (3) allocation of resources to support nonnegotiable goals. These are viewed as necessary conditions for attainment of district goals for achievement and instruction. The complexities of collaborative goal setting are many including strained relations with teacher unions. However, the necessity of including all significant stakeholders in the design of district goals was highlighted. Board alignment was discussed in the historical context of its changing role and perceptions. Finally, resource allocation was discussed in the context of how other countries allocate their resources. Recommendations were provided for each area.

6 Defined Autonomy in a High-Reliability District

Ultimately, the combined findings from our study boil down to a simple generalization—districts should seek to become high-reliability organizations regarding student achievement and effective instruction. While simple in its directness, this generalization when implemented changes the nature of leadership at the district level (obviously) and at the school level (not so obviously). That is, a high-reliability district alters how principals approach leadership in their schools. In our book *School Leadership That Works* (Marzano et al., 2005), we reported on the findings from our analysis of sixty-nine studies on principal leadership. We found that principal leadership at the school level has a correlation of .25 with student achievement.

It is useful to contrast our findings regarding leadership at the school level with our findings regarding leadership at the district level. Recall from chapter 1 that the correlation between district leadership and student achievement at the district level is .24, whereas the correlation between school leadership and student achievement at the school level is .25. Given how close in value these correlations are, one might get the impression that leadership at the district level and leadership at the school level are the same. Strong leadership at the school affects student achievement the same way as strong leadership at the district. This would be a misimpression. In fact, leadership at the two levels can be at cross-purposes in terms of a district seeking high-reliability status. This was demonstrated by Snijders and Bosker (1999). To illustrate, consider figure 6.1 (page 88).

Figure 6.1 presents a hypothetical situation. The vertical axis represents student achievement. and the horizontal axis represents five districts: A, B, C, D, and E. Here, the average achievement of students in District A is greater than the achievement of students in District B, the achievement of students in District B is greater than that of students in District C, and so on. One might think that District A is a high-reliability district and District E is not. In fact, none of the districts might be highly reliable. This is depicted in figure 6.2 (page 88).

In figure 6.2, we have added symbols for the schools within each district. In each case, there are five schools, and in each case, there is considerable variation in the

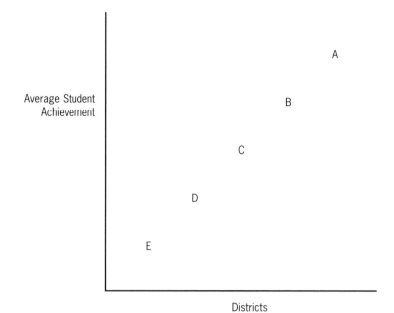

Figure 6.1 Average achievement for five districts

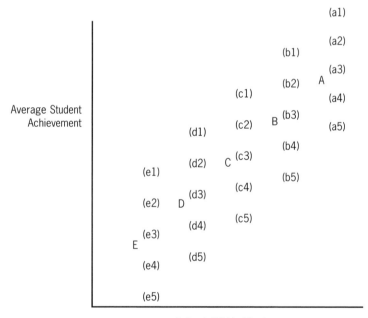

Figure 6.2 Achievement for schools within districts

achievement of students from school to school. For example, consider the five schools in District A (School a1, School a2, School a3, School a4, and School a5). It has a high-performing school (a1) and a relatively low-performing school (a5). Contrast this with the five schools in District E. It too has a school performing reasonably well (School e1), although not as well as the schools in District A. While it is true that, in general, the achievement of schools in District A is higher than the achievement of schools in District E, both districts have substantial variation in the achievement of their students across schools. Neither are high-reliability organizations when it comes to student achievement. In fact, none of the districts depicted in figure 6.2 report high-reliability status regarding achievement. A set of high-reliability districts would have profiles like those depicted in figure 6.3.

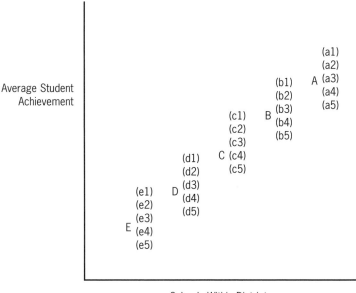

Figure 6.3 Profile of a high-reliability district: less variability between schools

In figure 6.3, there is still variability in the achievement of schools within districts. However, the variability is far less than that depicted in figure 6.2. It is a short step from this illustration to the realization that district leadership in a highly reliable district decreases the variability of the leadership across schools in the district. This in essence is what we mean by *defined autonomy*. Building leaders must lead within the confines of the nonnegotiable district goals for achievement and instruction and the constraints those goals place on principal leadership autonomy at the school level. How exactly might this look?

The Common Work of Schools Within a District

In chapter 1, we introduced our "surprising and perplexing finding" that we reconciled with the concept of defined autonomy. On one hand, we found evidence that school autonomy has a positive relationship with student achievement. On the other hand, we found little or no relationship between site-based management and student achievement. This seeming paradox is rendered less mysterious through the construct of defined autonomy. While it is true that schools are unique and must operate in such a way as to address their unique needs, it is also true that each school must operate as a functional component of a larger system. It is the larger system—the district—that establishes the common work of schools within the district, and it is that common work that becomes the "glue" holding the district together.

Elmore (2003) contends that the selection a school makes regarding its work (that is, what to work on next) is perhaps the most critical factor in the school's ability to improve student achievement. In a study commissioned by the National Governors Association, Elmore states that "knowing the right thing to do is the central problem of school improvement" (p. 9). He further notes that there is a perception in the United States that "schools fail because the people in them—administrators, teachers, and students—don't work hard enough and they are lazy, unmotivated, and self-serving" (p. 9). As a result of Elmore's analyses of low-performing schools, he concluded that this perception is inaccurate. In fact, failing schools are frequently populated by administrators, teachers, and students who work hard. However, they do not select the *right* work. Their efforts, as Herculean as they might be, produce little results in terms of student achievement.

Based on our findings, we assert that in a high-reliability district, the *right work* in every school is defined (at least in part) by the district—every student will demonstrate high achievement as a result of access to high-quality instruction. This common focus for schools within a district is supported by Robinson's (2007) meta-analysis of school-level behaviors or *dimensions* that have a statistically significant association with enhanced student achievement. Although she uses terminology different from ours, she concludes that clear goals regarding student achievement and effective instruction undertaken at the school level are among the most powerful actions schools can take. We add the notion that such goals should be established at the district level as nonnegotiable at the school level.

School Leadership for Defined Autonomy

Given that nonnegotiable goals for achievement and instruction are the right work for every school in a high-reliability district, each principal must operate in the context of these goals. This perspective necessarily qualifies the findings from our study on principal leadership. In the book *School Leadership That Works* (2005), we identified twenty-one leadership responsibilities for school-level administrators. These are listed in table 6.1 (pages 91–93).

Table 6.1 Twenty-One Principal Leadership Responsibilities

Responsibilities	The Extent to Which the Principal . . .	Specific Practices
Culture	Fosters shared beliefs and a sense of community and cooperation	• Promotes cooperation among staff • Promotes a sense of well-being • Promotes cohesion among staff • Develops an understanding of purpose • Develops a shared vision of what the school could be like
Order	Establishes a set of standard operating procedures and routines	• Provides and enforces clear structure, rules, and procedures for students • Provides and enforces clear structures, rules, and procedures for staff • Establishes routines regarding the running of the school that staff understand and follow
Discipline	Protects teachers from issues and influences that would detract from their teaching time or focus	• Protects instructional time from interruptions • Protects teachers from distractions
Resources	Provides teachers with materials and professional development necessary for the successful execution of their jobs	• Ensures teachers have necessary materials and equipment • Ensures teachers have necessary staff development opportunities that directly enhance their teaching
Involvement in curriculum, instruction, and assessment	Is directly involved in the design and implementation of curriculum, instruction, and assessment practices	• Is involved in helping teachers design curricular activities • Is involved with teachers to address instructional issues in their classrooms • Is involved with teachers to address assessment issues
Focus	Establishes clear goals and keeps those goals in the forefront of the school's attention	• Establishes high, concrete goals and expectations that all students meet them • Establishes concrete goals for all curriculum, instruction, and assessment • Establishes concrete goals for the general functioning of the school • Continually keeps attention on established goals
Knowledge of curriculum, instruction, and assessment	Is knowledgeable about current curriculum, instruction, and assessment practices	• Is knowledgeable about instructional practices • Is knowledgeable about assessment practices • Provides conceptual guidance for teachers regarding effective classroom practice
Visibility	Has quality contact and interactions with teachers and students	• Makes systematic frequent visits to classrooms • Maintains high visibility around the school • Has frequent contact with students

continued on next page ▶

Responsibilities	The Extent to Which the Principal . . .	Specific Practices
Contingent rewards	Recognizes and rewards individual accomplishments	• Recognizes individuals who excel • Uses performance rather than seniority as the primary criterion for reward and advancement • Uses hard work and results as the basis for reward and recognition
Communication	Establishes strong lines of communication with teachers and among students	• Is easily accessible to teachers • Develops effective means for teachers to communicate with one another • Maintains open and effective lines of communication with staff
Outreach	Is an advocate and spokesperson for the school to all stakeholders	• Assures the school is in compliance with district and state mandates • Advocates on behalf of the school in the community • Advocates for the school with parents • Ensures the central office is aware of the school's accomplishments
Input	Involves teachers in the design and implementation of important decisions and policies	• Provides opportunity for input on all important decisions • Provides opportunities for staff to be involved in developing school policies • Uses the leadership team in decision making
Affirmation	Recognizes and celebrates school accomplishments and acknowledges failures	• Systematically and fairly recognizes and celebrates accomplishments of teachers • Systematically and fairly recognizes and celebrates accomplishments of students • Systematically acknowledges failures and celebrates accomplishments of the school
Relationships	Demonstrates an awareness of the personal aspects of teachers and staff	• Remains aware of personal needs of teachers • Maintains personal relationships with teachers • Is informed about significant personal issues within the lives of staff members • Acknowledges significant events in the lives of staff members
Change agent	Is willing to and actively challenges the status quo	• Consciously challenges the status quo • Is comfortable with leading change initiatives with uncertain outcomes • Systematically considers new and better ways of doing things
Optimizer	Inspires and leads new and challenging innovations	• Inspires teachers to accomplish things that might seem beyond their grasp • Portrays a positive attitude about the ability of the staff to accomplish substantial things • Is a driving force behind major initiatives

Responsibilities	The Extent to Which the Principal . . .	Specific Practices
Ideals/beliefs	Communicates and operates from strong ideals and beliefs about schooling	• Holds strong professional beliefs about schools, teaching, and learning • Shares beliefs about schools, teaching, and learning with the staff • Demonstrates behaviors that are consistent with beliefs
Monitors/ evaluates	Monitors the effectiveness of school practices and their impact on student learning	• Monitors and evaluates the effectiveness of curriculum, instruction, and assessment
Flexibility	Adapts his or her leadership behavior to the needs of the current situation and is comfortable with dissent	• Is comfortable with major changes in how things are done • Encourages people to express opinions contrary to those with authority • Adapts leadership style to the needs of specific situations • Can be directive or nondirective as the situation warrants
Intellectual stimulation	Ensures faculty and staff are aware of the most current theories and practices and makes the discussion of these a regular aspect of the school's culture	• Keeps informed about current research and theory regarding effective schooling • Continually exposes the staff to cutting-edge ideas about how to be effective • Systematically engages staff in discussions about current research and theory • Continually involves the staff in reading articles and books about effective practices
Situational awareness	Is aware of the details and undercurrents in the running of the school and uses this information to address current and potential problems	• Is aware of informal groups and relationships among staff of the school • Is aware of issues in the school that have not surfaced but could create discord • Can predict what could go wrong from day to day

In the context of defined autonomy, the twenty-one responsibilities listed in table 6.1 must be recontextualized and redefined. Table 6.2 (page 94) lists the school-level responsibilities categorized by the district-level initiative that most strongly affects and redefines them. We then discuss how each district-level initiative redefines specific school leadership responsibilities.

Table 6.2 District-Level Initiatives Affecting School-Level Responsibilities

District-Level Initiative	School-Level Responsibilities Affected by District-Level Initiative
Ensure collaborative goal setting	• Input • Communication • Ideals and beliefs • Culture • Situational awareness • Change agent
Establish nonnegotiable goals for achievement and instruction	• Focus • Outreach • Order • Intellectual stimulation • Knowledge of curriculum, instruction, and assessment • Involvement in curriculum, instruction, and assessment
Create board alignment and support	• Outreach • Flexibility
Monitor nonnegotiable goals	• Monitor and evaluate • Flexibility • Optimizer • Affirmation • Contingent rewards
Allocate resources	• Resources

District Initiative: Ensure Collaborative Goal Setting

As depicted in table 6.2, the district initiative for collaborative goal setting affects how principals carry out the following school-level responsibilities:

- Input

- Communication

- Ideals and beliefs

- Culture

- Situational awareness

- Change agent

At the school level, the responsibility *input* means the principal makes sure that teachers have input into major decisions. In the context of collaborative goal setting at the district level, *input* must be reinterpreted as meaning that the principal makes sure teachers are aware of the decisions being made at the district level regarding non-negotiable goals for achievement and instruction. Additionally, the principal must act as the voice of the teachers during district meetings. Within a building, the principal and teachers discuss the deliberations at the district level (as reported by the principal) and collectively develop a schoolwide position. The principal then becomes the voice of the school at district-level goal-setting meetings.

At the school level, the responsibility *communication* means the principal is accessible to staff and the community and that staff members have access to one another. This dynamic is particularly important during the district's collaborative goal-setting process. Teachers must have the invitation and means to communicate with the principal formally and informally about their concerns regarding district initiatives. This will help the principal to obtain a clear understanding of the position of the teachers in his or her building so that the principal can represent that position at district-level meetings.

At the school level, the responsibility *ideals and beliefs* means the principal not only articulates his or her beliefs about teaching and learning but also models them for others. Additionally, the school as a whole develops a shared set of ideals and beliefs from which they operate. Again, this is particularly important during collaborative goal setting at the district level. The principal must voice and operate from the school's shared ideals and beliefs at district meetings. A basic goal of the principal should be that nonnegotiable district goals are developed in a manner consistent with building-level ideals and beliefs.

The school-level responsibility *culture* means the principal works with the staff to develop a shared vision of possibilities for their school. During collaborative goal setting, the principal's role is twofold relative to this responsibility—to ensure that a meaningful, shared vision is constructed at the school and to ensure that the school-level vision incorporates the district-level vision as manifested by the nonnegotiable goals for achievement and instruction. This is not to say that the school must simply adopt the district's vision. Rather, the school might augment district goals for achievement and instruction by identifying additions that meet their specific needs and dispositions.

In a school, the responsibility *situational awareness* means the principal remains aware of what is going well and what could go wrong from day to day in the school. Specifically, principals should remain aware of local opinion leaders. Awareness of which staff and local community members are viewed by others as opinion leaders is always critical, inasmuch as these are the people whose responses to ideas can accelerate or obstruct adoption of a new initiative. During collaborative goal setting at the district level, the principal needs to stay connected to local opinion leaders to frame district initiatives in a way that speaks to local needs and to listen to the views of local opinion leaders regarding district initiatives.

The school-level responsibility *change agent* means the principal challenges the status quo in the school when necessary. If designed and executed well, the district's collaborative goal-setting process should challenge the status quo for every school in the system. When the district goal-setting process produces goals that push the system, principals are equipped with challenges to the status quo. No longer can a school operate in isolation of other schools. Rather, each school is challenged to function as a working component within a larger system that is dedicated to high levels of achievement for all students.

District Initiative: Establish Nonnegotiable Goals for Achievement and Instruction

Nonnegotiable district goals for achievement and instruction affect how principals carry out the following school-level responsibilities:

- Focus

- Outreach

- Order

- Intellectual stimulation

- Knowledge of curriculum, instruction, and assessment

- Involvement in curriculum, instruction, and assessment

At the school level, *focus* means the principal establishes clear and measurable goals for the school. The link between the responsibility of focus and district-level goals for achievement and instruction is fairly obvious. In a district in which the board has adopted nonnegotiable goals for achievement and instruction, the principal's job is to ensure that his school adopts school goals that are clear, measurable school-level equivalents of the district's goals.

The school-level responsibility *outreach* means the principal is a spokesperson and advocate for the school to the district and the community; he or she ensures that school initiatives are aligned with state and district mandates. In a district with nonnegotiable goals for achievement and instruction, fulfilling this responsibility means that the principal communicates to the district and the community how the school is fulfilling the district goals in a way that meets the unique needs of the school. The principal's outreach efforts are focused on keeping district leaders and community members well informed about the school's adoption and adaptation of district goals.

The school-level responsibility *order* means the principal establishes predictable routines with supporting structures and systems. In the context of the district's goals for achievement and instruction, the principal must view this responsibility as foundational.

That is, the principal must ensure that the school maintains a safe and orderly climate so that the district's goals regarding achievement and instruction can be accomplished. The order (or lack thereof) maintained by each principal communicates to teachers that the district goals will result in an efficient, well-functioning school.

The school-level responsibility *intellectual stimulation* means the principal makes teachers aware of the latest research and theories on teaching and learning and the implications of that research and theory for classroom practice. In the context of district goals for achievement and instruction, this responsibility necessarily focuses on current research and theory regarding the district goals for achievement and instruction. Specifically, bolstered by resources and training provided by the district, the principal should inform teachers in his or her building on the research and theory supporting nonnegotiable goals for achievement and instruction. This would include research and theory regarding the advantages of a school being part of a high-reliability organization as opposed to operating as an autonomous unit.

At the school level, the responsibility *knowledge of curriculum, instruction, and assessment* means that the principal is knowledgeable about general practices regarding curriculum, instruction, and assessment. Within the framework of district goals for achievement and instruction, this responsibility narrows. All principals throughout the district must possess in-depth knowledge of the district's goals and how those goals will affect the lives of teachers. This knowledge should enable the principal to explain to teachers in their buildings how these district initiatives will affect their daily lives regarding curriculum, instruction, and assessment.

The school-level responsibility *involvement in curriculum, instruction, and assessment* means the principal is able to work side-by-side with teachers while they are engaged in classroom curriculum design, instructional planning, analyzing formative achievement data, and examining samples of student work. In a district with nonnegotiable goals for achievement and instruction, this "hands-on" work addresses how curriculum, instruction, and assessment must be structured to address district goals. Working side-by-side with teachers, the principal grapples with changes that must be made in the daily practice of curriculum, instruction, and assessment to meet district goals.

District Initiative: Create Board Alignment and Support

Board alignment and support affect how principals carry out the following responsibilities:

- Outreach

- Flexibility

The school-level responsibility *outreach* was discussed previously in relationship to the district-level responsibility of nonnegotiable goals for achievement and instruction.

The point was made that principals fulfill this responsibility as they align school goals with district goals. The responsibility of outreach is also fulfilled as principals advocate for district goals within their local community. In the context of board alignment and support, the principal is also responsible for keeping the board aware of pockets of support and pockets of dissent for district goals within their local communities. Such information helps the board make necessary corrections to ensure the success of district initiatives.

At the school level, the responsibility *flexibility* means that principals adapt their leadership styles based on the situation and needs of staff and community. In the context of the board alignment and support, this responsibility is effectively fulfilled when principals know when to answer questions of staff and community members and when to simply listen to their concerns, when to apply pressure to groups of people and when to relieve pressure, and when to "step up" and be out in front of an issue and when to "step back" and ask others to take charge. Such actions make it easier for school board members to align with and support district goals since building principals are defusing many potential problems through a flexible approach to leadership at the school level.

District Initiative: Monitor Nonnegotiable Goals

Monitoring nonnegotiable goals affects how principals carry out the following responsibilities:

- Monitor and evaluate

- Flexibility

- Optimizer

- Affirmation

- Contingent rewards

The school-level responsibility of *monitor and evaluate* is mediated by the district responsibility of monitoring nonnegotiable goals for achievement and instruction. In this case, principals must keep district-level leadership informed about the quality, fidelity, intensity, and consistency of implementation of the district's instructional goals. They must also monitor and evaluate the effect of the district's instructional goals on teachers and on students. Coordinating the responsibility of monitoring and evaluating between the school and district levels provides the superintendent and school board formative data on the status of district initiatives.

The district-level responsibility of monitoring nonnegotiable goals has implications for the school-level responsibility *flexibility* that was discussed earlier in relationship to board alignment and support. In the context of the district initiative to monitor nonnegotiable goals for achievement and instruction, this school-level responsibility translates to midcourse corrections at the district level. As the district makes changes to its goals because of feedback from the field, the principal makes necessary adaptations to school-level activities.

The school-level responsibility *optimizer* means the principal inspires hope and resilience among the staff and community. Hope and resilience are strengthened as the principal interprets successes and disappointments in school performance. The district-level responsibility monitoring nonnegotiable goals will bring attention to individual and collective school-level successes. As an optimizer, the principal must consistently be an advocate for the district initiatives. This is particularly important when teachers within a school begin to focus on the negative aspects of district initiatives or are going through the "implementation dip" associated with many innovations.

The school-level responsibility *affirmation* means the principal acknowledges school successes as well as failures. At the school level, such dialogue focuses on school efforts in isolation. In the context of the district initiative of monitoring goals for achievement and instruction, school successes and failures are addressed in a much broader context. The principal seeks to explore how school successes are aided or hindered by district initiatives. The same approach is taken with school failures. Each is examined in light of the influence of district-level initiatives. This information is fed back to district leaders so that appropriate corrections can be made.

While the school-level responsibility affirmation focuses on group or collective recognition, the school-level responsibility *contingent rewards* means the principal recognizes individual contributions to success. Monitoring goals at the district level should provide opportunities to reward individual contributions to the success of district goals. Rewards in this case may be as simple as a private expression of thanks or as formal and tangible as public ceremonies and/or financial incentives.

District Initiative: Allocate Resources

The district-level initiative regarding allocating resources has an obvious and straightforward relationship with the school-level responsibility of *resources*. The school-level responsibility means the principal allocates school resources to ensure that teachers have access to essential instructional materials and receive effective professional development regarding the programs and initiatives identified by the school. With the identification of district goals for achievement and instruction, individual schools have fewer degrees of freedom regarding how resources are expended. Now each principal must ensure that school resources are expended in such a way as to directly enhance the attainment of district goals regarding achievement and instruction.

As the preceding discussion illustrates, the twenty-one responsibilities associated with effective principal leadership identified in *School Leadership That Works* (Marzano et al., 2005) must be reconceptualized in the context of defined autonomy that is characteristic of a high-reliability district. Table 6.3 (pages 100–102) summarizes the preceding discussion by contrasting the twenty-one principal leadership responsibilities in a high-reliability district with the twenty-one responsibilities enacted in a district that does not practice defined autonomy. Note that three principal responsibilities are not influenced by district initiatives. They are (1) discipline, (2) visibility, and (3) relationships. Each of these deals with behaviors that are idiosyncratic to the people within a specific school, their routines, and interactions.

Table 6.3 Twenty-One Principal Responsibilities in Highly Reliable Districts

Responsibility	Characteristics in a District That Does Not Practice Defined Autonomy	Characteristics in a High-Reliability District
Culture	• Promotes cooperation among staff • Promotes a sense of well-being • Promotes cohesion among staff • Develops an understanding of purpose • Develops a shared vision of what the school could be like	• Ensures that district goals are incorporated in the school's shared vision • Keeps the district-level goals in the forefront of discussions of school vision
Order	• Provides and enforces clear structure, rules, and procedures for students • Provides and enforces clear structures, rules, and procedures for staff • Establishes routines regarding the running of the school that staff understand and follow	• Provides a safe and orderly environment as a foundation for district initiatives
Discipline	• Protects instructional time from interruptions • Protects teachers from distractions	Remains the same
Resources	• Ensures teachers have necessary materials and equipment • Ensures teachers have necessary staff development opportunities that directly enhance their teaching	• Ensures that teachers have necessary materials, equipment, and staff development to carry out district initiatives
Involvement in curriculum, instruction, and assessment	• Is involved in helping teachers design curricular activities • Is involved with teachers to address instructional issues in their classrooms • Is involved with teachers to address assessment issues	• Works side-by-side with teachers to ensure that curriculum, instruction, and assessment activities are aligned with district goals
Focus	• Establishes high, concrete goals and expectations that all students meet them • Establishes concrete goals for all curriculum, instruction, and assessment • Establishes concrete goals for the general functioning of the school • Continually keeps attention on established goals	• Ensures that the school adopts local goals that are in alignment with district goals
Knowledge of curriculum, instruction, and assessment	• Is knowledgeable about instructional practices • Is knowledgeable about assessment practices • Provides conceptual guidance for teachers regarding effective classroom practice	• Possesses in-depth knowledge of how the district goals will affect the day-to-day lives of teachers

Responsibility	Characteristics in a District That Does Not Practice Defined Autonomy	Characteristics in a High-Reliability District
Visibility	• Makes systematic frequent visits to classrooms • Maintains high visibility around the school • Has frequent contact with students	Remains the same
Contingent rewards	• Recognizes individuals who excel • Uses performance versus seniority as the primary criterion for reward and advancement • Uses hard work and results as the basis for reward and recognition	• Applies rewards that pertain to accomplishing district goals within the school
Communication	• Is easily accessible to teachers • Develops effective means for teachers to communicate with one another • Maintains open and effective lines of communication with staff	• Provides opportunities for teachers to communicate concerns about district initiatives
Outreach	• Assures the school is in compliance with district and state mandates • Advocates on behalf of the school in the community • Advocates for the school with parents • Ensures the central office is aware of the school's accomplishments	• Communicates to the district how the school is fulfilling district initiatives in a way that meets the unique needs of the school • Advocates for school and district goals with opinion leaders
Input	• Provides opportunity for input on all important decisions • Provides opportunities for staff to be involved in developing school policies • Uses the leadership team in decision making	• Makes sure teachers are aware of decisions made at the district level • Becomes the voice of the school in district decisions
Affirmation	• Systematically and fairly recognizes and celebrates accomplishments of teachers • Systematically and fairly recognizes and celebrates accomplishments of students • Systematically acknowledges failures and celebrates accomplishments of the school	• Explores how school success and failures are influenced by district initiatives
Relationships	• Remains aware of personal needs of teachers • Maintains personal relationships with teachers • Is informed about significant personal issues within the lives of staff members • Acknowledges significant events in the lives of staff members	Remains the same
Change agent	• Consciously challenges the status quo • Is comfortable with leading change initiatives with uncertain outcomes • Systematically considers new and better ways of doing things	• Translates and communicates district goals in a way that challenges the status quo of the school

continued on next page ▶

Responsibility	Characteristics in a District That Does Not Practice Defined Autonomy	Characteristics in a High-Reliability District
Optimizer	• Inspires teachers to accomplish things that might seem beyond their grasp • Portrays a positive attitude about the ability of the staff to accomplish substantial things • Is a driving force behind major initiatives	• Consistently advocates for district initiatives particularly when teachers begin to focus on negative consequences
Ideals/beliefs	• Holds strong professional beliefs about schools, teaching, and learning • Shares beliefs about schools, teaching, and learning with the staff • Demonstrates behaviors that are consistent with beliefs	• Represents ideals and beliefs of the school during district meetings
Monitors/evaluates	• Monitors and evaluates the effectiveness of curriculum, instruction, and assessment	• Keeps district-level leadership informed about the quality, fidelity, and implementation of district initiatives
Flexibility	• Is comfortable with major changes in how things are done • Encourages people to express opinions contrary to those with authority • Adapts leadership style to the needs of specific situations • Can be directive or nondirective as the situation warrants	• Maintains appropriate balance between listening and intervening when problems occur regarding district initiatives • Makes changes to schoolwide activities based on changes in district initiatives
Intellectual stimulation	• Keeps informed about current research and theory regarding effective schooling • Continually exposes the staff to cutting-edge ideas about how to be effective • Systematically engages staff in discussions about current research and theory • Continually involves the staff in reading articles and books about effective practices	• Makes teachers aware of research and theory supporting district initiatives as well as research and theory supporting the efficacy of highly reliable districts
Situational awareness	• Is aware of informal groups and relationships among staff of the school • Is aware of issues in the school that have not surfaced but could create discord • Can predict what could go wrong from day to day	• Maintains awareness of local opinion leaders in the community with respect to district initiatives

The changes in school leadership practices necessitated within a district seeking the status of a high-reliability organization put the concept of defined autonomy in sharp focus. Principals within the districts and teachers within buildings no longer can behave as autonomous entities. All operate in the context of nonnegotiable district goals for achievement and instruction. This is not to say that principals and teachers are not free to try innovative approaches to district goals. Indeed, such creativity is central to the *autonomy* part of *defined autonomy*.

Summary and Conclusions

This chapter addressed the concept of defined autonomy. This is a critical operating principle for a district seeking high-reliability status. Defined autonomy is operationalized in terms of the leadership behaviors of principals. Specifically, the twenty-one responsibilities of a principal (identified in a previous study) must be redefined or reconceptualized when a district seeks to be a high-reliability organization.

7 The Perils and Promises of Second-Order Change

The previous chapters have described concrete initiatives districts must engage in to move toward the status of a high-reliability organization. This chapter addresses the types of changes these initiatives require in a district. Specifically, we believe that the initiatives discussed in this book constitute second-order change for the vast majority of districts in the United States.

In the book *School Leadership That Works* (Marzano et al., 2005), we addressed the contrast between first-order change and second-order change. In different terminology, others have discussed this same distinction (Argyris & Schön, 1974, 1978; Heifetz, 1994). Table 7.1 outlines some critical differences or distinctions regarding first-order change and second-order change.

Table 7.1 Characteristics of First-Order Change and Second-Order Change

First-Order Change	Second-Order Change
• Is perceived as an extension of the past	• Is perceived as a break with the past
• Fits within existing paradigms	• Lies outside existing paradigms
• Is consistent with prevailing values and norms	• Conflicts with prevailing values and norms
• Can be implemented with existing knowledge and skills	• Requires the acquisition of new knowledge and skills
• Requires resources currently available to those responsible for implementing the innovations	• Requires resources currently not available to those responsible for implementing the innovations
• May be accepted because of common agreement that the innovation is necessary	• May be resisted because only those who have a broad perspective of the school see the innovation as necessary

The first distinction listed in table 7.1 is the extent to which a proposed change is perceived as an extension of or break from the past. Changes that are perceived as extensions of the past are usually first order in magnitude; changes that are perceived as breaks with the past are usually second order. On the surface, nonnegotiable district-level goals for achievement might seem like an extension of the past. Ever since the initiation of

NCLB, districts have been concerned about student achievement. However, the specific recommendations made in chapter 3 involving standards-based report cards would be a break from the past in the vast majority of U.S. districts. This is because assigning grades as described in chapter 3 follows a uniform process and is not left up to the idiosyncratic practices of individual teachers. One might argue that whenever you try to change grading policies, you are tinkering with aspects of schooling that some consider sacred. About this issue, Olson (1995) notes that the use of grades "is one of the most sacred traditions in American education . . . The truth is that grades have acquired an almost cult-like importance in American schools. They are the primary shorthand tools for communicating to parents how children are faring" (p. 24).

Nonnegotiable goals for instruction also break from the past in most districts. Indeed, the norm throughout the country is that teachers have very little if any accountability for the effectiveness of their teaching, particularly in terms of student learning (see Millman, 1997). A districtwide move to ensuring *effective teaching* (defined as student knowledge gain brought about by the use of effective teaching strategies) in every classroom would certainly be viewed as a dramatic break from the past in many districts.

The second distinction in table 7.1 addresses whether a proposed change fits within existing paradigms or lies outside of existing paradigms. Given that districts as currently configured are not high-reliability organizations regarding achievement and instruction, the changes proposed in this book are by definition second order in nature. Attaining and monitoring high levels of achievement for all students by ensuring effective teaching in every classroom flies in the face of the current mode of operations for most U.S. districts. While many schools have taken on this challenge of enhancing student achievement, few districts have ventured into this level of accountability.

The third distinction in table 7.1 involves the extent to which a proposed change is consistent with prevailing values and norms or conflicts with prevailing values and norms. Of all the distinctions listed in table 7.1, this might be the most malleable. Certainly one can make a case that prevailing norms and values in most districts probably conflict with many of the changes suggested in this text. However, values and norms can be influenced. Changing existing norms and values within a district might be one of the primary leadership opportunities for districts wishing to be high-reliability organizations with regard to achievement and instruction.

The fourth distinction in table 7.1 focuses on the extent to which a proposed change can be accomplished with existing knowledge and skills. While the knowledge regarding how to monitor achievement expressed in metrics of knowledge gain has been available in the theoretical and research literature for years (see the discussion in chapter 3) as has been the knowledge necessary to provide effective instruction in every classroom (see the discussion in chapter 4), this knowledge base has not filtered down to the classroom level. Indeed, the impotence of information is one of the defining features of a loosely coupled system—information has little impact on the actual running of the system.

Consequently, the efforts needed to provide every teacher in a district with training in the specifics of the nonnegotiable goals for achievement and instruction (as outlined in chapters 3 and 4) would most likely be a second-order challenge in most districts.

The fifth distinction in table 7.1 addresses whether a proposed change requires resources that are currently available to those responsible for implementing the innovation. Available resources make for first-order change; unavailable resources make for second-order change. While the general information necessary to establish nonnegotiable goals for achievement and instruction is certainly available, monetary resources would have to be reallocated to provide the time and training necessary to implement these innovations. This was discussed in chapter 5. There, we noted that few if any other initiatives should be occurring in a district other than nonnegotiable goals for achievement and instruction. Stated differently, district goals for achievement and instruction must be the first priority in terms of resource allocation. In some (or perhaps many) districts, there might be few if any leftover resources for other initiatives. This level of focus and discipline might be considered by many in a district as second-order change.

The final distinction listed in table 7.1 addresses whether there is agreement that a proposed change is necessary. Given that individual classroom teachers are rarely privy to a holistic view of district initiatives and the reasoning behind these initiatives, it is probably unlikely that teachers within a district would readily acknowledge the need for nonnegotiable goals for achievement and instruction at the district level. This same issue is addressed by Flinders (1988) in his article "Teacher Isolation and the New Reform." He notes that teacher isolation is an adaptive strategy teachers engage in because of the cellular organization of schools which are unwittingly designed to minimize interaction. Unfortunately, the by-product of this isolation is a myopic view on the part of teachers. They see as useful or necessary only those things that will positively affect their daily lives. Additionally, they have a bias toward maintaining the status quo. Any change that would disrupt their established routine, even if only in the short run, most likely will be viewed as negative.

Living Through the Tough Times

From the previous discussion, it is easy to conclude that nonnegotiable district goals for achievement and instruction must be addressed as second-order change. This poses problems for district-level leaders. One critical finding in our analysis of school-level leadership (Marzano et al., 2005) was that during second-order change, leadership can expect some individuals within the system to complain that things have become worse as a result of the new innovation. We believe there are some corollaries between our findings regarding leadership at the school level and leadership at the district level specifically when it comes to second-order change.

Just as school principals must live through some difficult times during second-order change, so too must district leaders. For example, during second-order change, school leaders will likely be faced with the perception by some faculty members that life is more chaotic in the schools and less ordered. So too will district leaders when engaged in second-order change. When nonnegotiable goals for achievement and instruction are implemented, it is highly likely that some principals might believe that the district runs less smoothly than before these innovations were instituted.

During second-order change, school principals will likely be faced with the perception that communication has broken down and a preexisting culture of cooperation has been disrupted. When nonnegotiable district goals for achievement and instruction have been implemented, district leadership might experience the same reactions from building-level leaders.

During second-order change, school leaders might face the perception from their staff that teachers have lost their voice regarding decisions about the school policy. The same phenomenon might be faced at the district level. Even when district leadership has taken great pains to ensure a collaborative decision-making process, some principals might view the nonnegotiable goals regarding achievement and instruction as a top-down decision obtained with little input from building principals.

As the preceding discussion illustrates, second-order change at the district level will most likely be accompanied by perceptions that "things" have gotten worse. If district leadership allows such perceptions to lessen their resolve or slow down their efforts to implement nonnegotiable goals for achievement and instruction, little progress will be made. Rather, district leadership must be willing to traverse the turbulent and some-times treacherous waters of negative perceptions. Such journeys often require a toler-ance for ambiguity. Fullan (1993) alludes to this phenomenon:

> "Ready, fire, aim" is the more fruitful sequence if we want to take a linear snapshot of an organization undergoing major reform. Ready is important; there has to be some notion of direction, but it is kill-ing to bog down the process with vision, mission, and strategic plan-ning before you know enough about dynamic reality. Fire is action and inquiry where skills, clarity, and learning are fostered. Aim is crys-tallizing new beliefs, formulating mission and vision statements, and focusing strategic planning. Vision and strategic planning come later. (pp. 31–32)

The works of Hall, Hord, and Loucks regarding the concerns-based adoption model (CBAM) also shed light on this issue. Specifically, CBAM (Hall & Hord, 1987; Hall & Loucks, 1978; Hall, Loucks, Rutherford, & Newlove, 1975; Hord, Rutherford, Huling-Austin, & Hall, 1987) has shown that there are many stages to implement-ing major initiatives. In the beginning, ambiguity and concern about the disruption to personal routines are common. Over time, however, concern shifts to the effec-tive functioning of the organization. While nonnegotiable goals for achievement and instruction might generate negative perceptions in some in the short run, over time, they will produce a sense of unity and a pride in accomplishment that high achievement and high-quality instruction are the centerpiece of the district.

Some Advice for District Leaders

A well-accepted principle taught to Top Gun Navy fighter pilots is that the safest move when encountering an enemy during air-to-air combat is to "turn into the threat" (Driscoll, 2005). If a fighter pilot's first move is to turn away from an oncoming enemy plane, he or she loses sight of the situation and forfeits the ability to make necessary corrections in behavior. The same principle seems to apply to district leaders when faced with "threats" regarding their second-order change initiatives. Turning into a threat means being proactive regarding the change process. Here we provide some recommendations for proactive leadership that come not from our meta-analysis of the research on district leadership, but from our cumulative experience in working with districts and schools throughout the United States as well as our interpretation of the suggestions of others.

Recommendation #1: Know the Implications of Your Initiatives

District leadership must have an in-depth understanding of how their second-order change initiative will affect the lives of building administrators and teachers and then use this understanding to forecast and address potential problems. For example, consider the implementation of a standards-based report card that uses formative assessments as discussed in chapter 3. In many districts across the country, teachers currently have a great deal of freedom about what they will teach in a given class or at a given grade level. Once a standards-based report card is in place, this freedom is usurped. Given that teachers must report student achievement and knowledge gain on specific topics, they have little choice but to teach to these topics. This might cause considerable angst for some teachers. This issue should be anticipated and adequate steps taken before implementation of the new report cards to prepare teachers. This would be done through extensive professional development.

Recommendation #2: Maintain a Unified Front

District leaders must portray a positive, unified front relative to their second-order change initiatives. When building administrators or teachers express doubts about the new standards-based reporting system (see chapter 3) or the system of feedback to teachers regarding the impact of their instruction on student achievement (see chapter 4), district leadership must be ready and willing to articulate the benefits of these interventions. All members of the district leadership team must present a united, positive stance regarding the district initiatives. Indeed, district leadership must embrace the responsibility of continually inspiring administrators and teachers throughout the district regarding the importance of the changes being made and the potential benefits for students.

Recommendation #3: Keep the Big Ideas in the Forefront

District leadership must constantly remind school administrators and teachers of the beliefs and ideas that lead them to the district's second-order change initiatives. Standards-based report cards are not implemented to increase the record-keeping tasks of teachers. Rather, they are implemented to more quickly identify students having difficulty in learning important content and then provide those students with timely and specific help. Similarly, an instructional model that is used to identify teacher strengths and weaknesses is not instituted to micromanage teachers' instructional practices. Rather, it is intended to help provide teachers with a vehicle to continually hone their craft while allowing them the latitude to develop their unique style of teaching.

Recommendation #4: Use What Is Known About Acceptance of New Ideas

How to create an atmosphere in which radical ideas or innovations are adopted has been well documented by Everett Rogers (*Diffusion of Innovations,* 2003) through his research in multiple settings with diverse populations. Specifically, individuals are more likely to adopt an innovation or accept a new idea when they see in them the following four attributes:

1. *Relative advantage*—Stakeholders are more likely to adopt a new idea or an innovation when they understand it as better than what it replaces. Individuals need to understand *how* and *why* new ideas or innovations are better for them personally or for the people they care most about. Stated differently, new ideas are accepted if people can see either "what's in it for me" or "how the people I care most about are better served." Considering relative advantage in the example of standards-based grading (see chapter 3), district leadership should present this innovation in ways to help teachers see how its implementation might lighten their workload at key times during the year, produce grades that more accurately reflect the learning of their students, and reduce conflicts with students and parents. Focusing on students and parents, leaders might also present this innovation as not only more accurate regarding student achievement, but also more fair to students than traditional grades.

2. *Compatibility*—Stakeholders are more likely to adopt new ideas or innovations when they are viewed as compatible with personal values and prior experience. Stated differently, it helps if stakeholders can draw on prior learning or experience to understand the new idea or innovation. Considering compatibility in the example of standards-based report cards, district leadership might want to

present this initiative through the use of metaphors with which all stakeholders can relate. An example of a familiar metaphor to help establish the compatibility of standards-based grading could be the Boy Scouts or Girl Scouts. In these programs, clear and specific standards for earning merit badges and advancing in rank must be met at one level before moving on to the next. Individuals can achieve the highest goals in Scouting based on their dedication and individual performance. Individual performance is assessed and reported against standards rather than on a curve or in comparison to the performance of others. Other potentially useful metaphors to which teachers might relate are testing for a driver's license or fitness training and testing. In these examples, clear standards are set, performance is assessed, and records reflect current status rather than averages-over-time or comparisons of one individual's performance to another's.

3. *Trialability*—Pilot testing new ideas or innovations in safe low-stakes settings will increase the rate of their adoption. Just as people want to test drive a car before purchasing it, they want to "test drive" a new initiative before adopting it. Using the standards-based grading example, giving a few individuals the opportunity to test new protocols, metrics, data management tools, and reporting schemes will increase the rate of adoption of standards-based grading for the entire district.

4. *Evidence*—People are more likely to adopt an idea or innovation when the idea is associated with evidence that it works. Again, using the standards-based grading example, if district leaders present evidence that using this approach leads to early detection of students in need, timely intervention, and a more accurate profile of student learning and achievement, the likelihood of adoption of this initiative will be enhanced.

Recommendation #5: Communicate With "Sticky Messages"

In his best-selling book *The Tipping Point*, Malcolm Gladwell (2002) introduces the concept of "sticky messages." His premise is that ideas or innovations "catch on" because there is something about them that sticks with people. He develops a theory of social epidemics largely on this premise. Gladwell describes a social epidemic as leaderless change, or change from the bottom up.

Building on the conclusions of Gladwell, district leaders should develop sticky messages regarding nonnegotiable goals for achievement and instruction. In their book *Made to Stick* (2007), authors Chip Heath and Dan Heath offer a number of principles for developing such messages. One principle of sticky messages offered by Heath and Heath is simplicity. An illustration of their simplicity principle is the "commander's intent" message. The essence of the commander's intent message is to reduce complex ideas to their simplest and most concrete forms. The commander's intent is the last sentence a military commander might add to mission-specific orders. An example might be something like "the intent of tomorrow's mission is to take the hill overlooking the city." Using the example of standards-based report cards, district leadership might develop and communicate the following message: "The purposes of standards-based report cards are accuracy, support, and fairness for students and teachers."

Recommendation #6: Manage Personal Transitions

Bridges (1980) makes a distinction between *change* and *transition*. Simply put, change is external and transition is internal. Typically, changes in programs and practices, especially those that are second order, represent a *gain* for students, schools, or school districts, but they can be perceived as a *loss* for the people responsible for implementing them. In school districts, these people are teachers and principals who will inevitably experience personal transitions. Managing these personal transitions is as important for leaders to manage as is managing the change itself. What appears to a leader as resistance to change in recalcitrant individuals may actually be a result of poorly managed personal transitions with those individuals for whom the change is second order.

One key to managing the process of personal transitions is for leaders to treat the experience the same way they would the process of grieving. When leaders recognize that for some individuals in the district, second-order change represents significant personal loss (loss of expertise, loss of confidence, loss of relationships, and loss of status), they will respond as they would following the loss of loved ones. They will organize and schedule events intended to honor the past: the people and initiatives that helped move the organization forward. These events may be simple rituals that allow people to celebrate what helped them accomplish important past objectives. Bridges (1980) refers to these events as "ceremonial endings" that acknowledge practices, programs, procedures, or approaches that will be "left behind." These events should be scheduled for the same reasons that we schedule graduation ceremonies and funeral services. They help people honor the past, acknowledge that something has ended, and move on. Additionally, such events may be followed by a period of mourning, or what Bridges calls the "neutral zone." The neutral zone is a period of time when people are letting go of the past, accepting what has ended and what has started, assimilating new knowledge and skills, and building confidence in themselves and in the future.

To shorten the period of time people spend in the neutral zone, Bridges offers four *P*s to a new beginning:

- *Purpose*—People need to know *why* the organizational change(s) associated with their personal loss is necessary.

- *Picture*—People need a picture, image, or vision of what the future will be like as a result of the change(s) associated with their loss.

- *Plan*—People need to know the plans for implementing change(s) associated with their loss.

- *Part*—People need to know what part they can and will be asked to play in the future.

Knowing that an organization is changing even when the intended change is for all of the right reasons does not save people from personal transitions. Seeing the purpose, picture, plan, and part of the initiative can help people through their personal transition in less time, with less stress, and with greater productivity.

Revisiting the Bonus Finding

We end our discussion of second-order change by returning to our "bonus finding" regarding superintendent longevity. Recall the discussion in chapter 1; somewhat serendipitously, we found that the longevity of the superintendent's leadership in a district has a statistically significant relationship with student achievement. In light of the discussion in the previous chapters, this now makes some sense, particularly if a district is involved in second-order change. By definition, such changes take a great deal of time to fully mature. Unfortunately, the trend in superintendent tenure is not exceptionally long and in some cases is exceptionally short. To illustrate, Kerr (1988) cites the following example:

> One school system in Upstate New York had 13 superintendents in 15 years. When a staff development team from a nearby university visited the school system to introduce a new in-service training concept, teachers said they were tired of being trained every year to suit the new superintendent's priorities—only to find him gone by the next year. (p. 21)

Fortunately, Kerr's example is an extreme. The 2000 survey by the American Association of School Administrators (AASA; Glass et al., 2000) provides a more optimistic perspective. As of 2000, the exact number of superintendents is not known because in hundreds of very small districts, the superintendent is also a principal and is not counted when frequencies are tabulated. With this qualification noted, the AASA estimates the number to be 13,728. This is down from about 14,000 to 14,500 estimated in 1990 because small districts are moving more toward consolidation. The average age of superintendents is fifty-two, and most superintendents spend about fourteen to seventeen years on the job in about two to three districts. The average length of stay is about five to seven years in each district. This is in contrast to the perception that the tenure of superintendents is about two and a half years. Glass et al. (2000) explain: "This figure originated a decade ago in several articles about rapid turnover in the superintendencies of large urban districts. Since that time, the tenure figure has had a life of its own. Unfortunately, it has fostered a negative image of the superintendency" (p. v).

While an average tenure of five to seven years is much better than the perceived tenure of two and a half years, it might still not be enough. To illustrate, when studying the implementation of comprehensive school reform (CSR) models, Borman, Hewes, Overman, and Brown (2003) found the effect size for comprehensive interventions rose over time and suggest that it might take longer than a decade for the effects of a CSR model to stabilize. CSR models are focused on individual schools. Surely one can anticipate the same timeline for districtwide interventions such as nonnegotiable goals for achievement and instruction. Without consistent leadership from the superintendent, nonnegotiable goals for achievement and instruction have little chance of success.

The implications regarding hiring and retaining superintendents are clear. School boards and the local community should seek to provide an environment for superintendents that will make them want to spend a decade or more in one school district. Likewise, school boards and the local community should demand a commitment from superintendents to remain long enough to see major changes to their full implementation. Kerr (1988) notes,

> School boards should try to determine if a prospective superintendent views the school system as simply another rung in his career ladder, if he is looking to score some successes and then move up to a larger school system, or if he is willing to expend his energy developing a long range agenda, implementing it, and sticking around long enough to evaluate the results. (p. 21)

Just as the district and community must make a commitment to the superintendent, the superintendent must make a commitment to the district. As Kerr notes, the superintendent must say, "This is my community, and I want to be superintendent here as long as I can be effective" (p. 21). Without such a commitment on the part of the superintendent, it is unwise and perhaps unfair to ask district personnel to engage in second-order change.

Epilogue

In his best-selling book *Collapse: How Societies Choose to Fail or Succeed,* University of California–Los Angeles anthropologist Jared Diamond (2005) reports his conclusion from a study of societies that failed, after surviving for long periods of time, in close proximity to societies that prospered. Among the societies he studied were the Anasazi Indians of the southwestern United States, Easter Island in the Pacific Rim, and the Norse Villages in Greenland. After surviving for centuries, each of these societies failed. They failed not because they were conquered by dominant competing societies or because they succumbed to new and unknown diseases. These societies failed because their members, particularly their leaders, perpetuated practices that led to their own demise. Typically, these were practices grounded in unexamined and deeply held beliefs. Quoting one of Diamond's seminal conclusions, "perhaps a crux of success or failure as a society is to know which core values to hold on to, and which ones to discard and replace with new values, when times change" (p. 433). Diamond arrives at this conclusion after examining numerous artifacts of these societies and recognizing the many opportunities leaders in them had to introduce new, adaptive, and more productive practices. Unfortunately, the fates of these societies were sealed by leaders who were unwilling to thoughtfully examine both beliefs and practices and consider more adaptive and effective alternatives. In each of these societies, beliefs distorted vision to the degree that leaders ignored evidence that could have "saved" their societies.

Diamond's conclusion about the failure of societies, in our view, applies as well to institutions and organizations. His statement about the success or failure of societies could easily be modified to read, the crux of success or failure of institutions and organizations is to know which practices to hold on to, and which ones to discard and replace with new practices, when times change. This is no less true for school- and district-level leaders than the leaders of ancient societies or other contemporary institutions and organizations. No one questions the pace, scope, and implications of change in today's world. Change is the one constant of which we can all be certain. The question for leaders in the middle of change is will there be improvement? More specifically, are leaders willing to examine their practices, even those grounded in deeply held beliefs, and consider alternatives likely to produce improved results?

In our studies of school- and district-level leadership, we have identified "value-added" leadership responsibilities and practices. That is, leadership practices that add value to the efforts of teachers and the learning of students. Skilled use of our findings and implementation of our recommendations will help school- and district-level leaders improve instructional quality for each student, in every classroom, everyday. Skilled use of our findings and implementation of our recommendations will help school- and district-level leaders reduce variability in the quality of instruction offered within schools and between schools. High instructional quality with low variability among teachers is a hallmark of the world's best-performing education systems. These attributes, high instructional quality with low variability both within-schools and between-schools, which are the keys to a high-reliability school district, do not exist in the absence of value-added leadership.

High instructional quality within and between schools, or increased reliability, is possible when school districts "strike the right balance" between direction and school support. School districts need *superior execution* from leaders at every level of the system on the responsibilities and practices presented in this and our earlier book, *School Leadership That Works*. The findings on which these books are based suggest that when value-added responsibilities are fulfilled through the practices we have identified, school district reliability increases, students are better served, and achievement is higher. So our final recommendations to district and school-level leaders are as follows:

- Take stock of your current practices and approaches. Use our findings and recommendations as a standard against which you assess your practices.

- Benchmark your use of these practices against implementation in the best-performing school districts in the world. Do not be content with existing levels of skill, assuming that levels of expertise are sufficient for high reliability. Dedicate yourselves to continuous improvement.

- Use our findings and recommendations as the foundation for your own professional development. There are many professional development options and resources available through McREL and other organizations; use them. Invest in the development of value-added leadership. It is clear from our findings that high-quality professional development for superintendents, school board members, district staff, and principals is closer to students and classrooms than most people think.

Our system of education is one of the most exciting experiments with the greatest promise in American history. It is also vulnerable. Like the societies studied by Jared Diamond, it can become a relic. We all want to avoid the specter of future educational historians or anthropologists dusting off artifacts of a failed American system of education and concluding, "If educational leaders had only known which practices to hold on to and which to discard in times of change, the system might have endured and delivered on its promise." Striking the right balance between district direction and school support, and superior execution of the responsibilities and practices we have presented, may be the difference between a failed system and one that delivers on the promise of opportunity and hope for all children through high-reliability education.

Technical Notes

Technical Note 1.1: Interpretation of Correlation Between Principal Leadership and Student Achievement

To interpret the .25 correlation between principal leadership and student achievement, assume that a principal is hired into a district and assigned to a school that is at the 50th percentile in terms of the average achievement of its students. Also assume that the principal is at the 50th percentile in terms of his leadership skills. All things remaining the same, one would predict that over time, school achievement would remain at the 50th percentile. But if one increases the principal's leadership skills by one standard deviation, the correlation of .25 indicates that over time, one would predict the average achievement of the school to rise to the 60th percentile.

This type of interpretation is used when a correlation coefficient is thought of in a predictive sense—the extent to which performance on one variable predicts performance on another variable. The equation representing this perspective is as follows:

$$(\text{Predicted } Z \text{ score}) = (\text{Predictor } Z \text{ score}) \times (\text{correlation})$$

The interpretation of this equation is grounded in the concept of a Z score. Using the preceding equation, we can predict the average achievement in a school in Z score form if we know the Z score for that school regarding the leadership behavior of the principal. For example, assume that a certain school has a Z score of 1.00 on the predictor variable which in this case is principal leadership behavior. Because the correlation between principal leadership behavior and student achievement has been computed to be .25, one multiplies the Z score of 1.00 on principal leadership by .25. Thus, the formula predicts that a school with a Z score of 1.00 on principal leadership behavior will have a Z score of .25 on the average academic achievement of students in the school.

Translating this into percentile terms, one can say that an increase in the predictor variable of one standard deviation is associated with an increase in the predicted variable from the 50th percentile to the 60th percentile because a Z score of .25 represents the 60th percentile on the unit normal distribution. It is important to note that when describing the relationship between an increase in leadership behavior and an increase in student achievement throughout the book, we have consistently used the term *associated with.* A correlation between two variables does not demonstrate a causal relationship between the two variables, although it does not exclude such a relationship.

Technical Note 1.2: General Methodology Used in This Study

There are a number of reasons a researcher might conduct a meta-analysis. Hunter and Schmidt (2004) cite three. Referring to the perspective taken by Glass (1976, 1977), they explain that one purpose is "simply to summarize and describe in a general way the studies in a research literature" (Hunter & Schmidt, 2004, p. 512). The second approach is attributed to Hedges and Olkin (1985) and Rosenthal (1984, 1991). This approach is more analytic in nature: "The focus is on examination of relationships between measures of particular constructs or between measures of specific types of treatments and measures of specific outcomes" (Hunter & Schmidt, 2004, p. 512). However, Hunter and Schmidt note that this approach is still focused on summarizing findings in a specific research literature. The third approach is that advocated by Hunter and Schmidt (2004). As described in the block quote in chapter 1, this approach is tantamount to asking and answering the question, what would be the relationship between district leadership and student achievement if all studies had been conducted perfectly (with no methodological limitations)? Operationally, this requires correction for study artifacts.

In a series of works, Hunter and Schmidt have detailed the rationale and importance of correcting for study artifacts (Hunter & Schmidt, 1990, 1994). They list a number of attenuation artifacts that alter the value of outcome measures making them imperfect estimates of relationships between variables. The artifacts that can be corrected include the following:

1. Sampling error

2. Error of measurement in the dependent variable

3. Error of measurement in the independent variable

4. Dichotomization of a continuous dependent variable

5. Dichotomization of a continuous independent variable

6. Range variation in the independent variable

7. Systematic attrition of subjects in the study from a specific interval of the continuum of the independent variable

8. Deviation from perfect construct validity in the independent variable

9. Deviation from perfect construct validity in the dependent variable

In the present study we corrected for two of these artifacts: (1) error of measurement in the dependent variable and (2) error of measurement in the independent variable. To illustrate, assume that the population correlation between district leadership behavior and student academic achievement is .50. A given study attempts to estimate that correlation but employs a measure of district leadership that has a reliability of .81. According to attenuation theory, this observed correlation will be reduced by a factor of .90 (the square root of the reliability). That is, the observed correlation will be .45 (.50 × .90) even if there is no attenuation because of the other artifacts listed by Hunter and Schmidt (2004). To correct an observed correlation for attenuation because of measurement error, one divides the observed correlation by the square of the reliability. In this case, the observed correlation of .45 would be divided by .90 (.45/.90 = .50).

If the study also employs a measure of the dependent variable (in this case, student achievement) that involves measurement error, then the observed correlation is even further from the true population value. Again, assume that the reliability of the dependent measure is .81. The observed correlation will be a function of both artifact attenuation factors or .90 × .90 × .50 = .405. Again, to correct the observed correlation of .405 for measurement error in the independent and dependent variables, one divides by the product of the square of the reliabilities or .81 (.90 × .90). Thus, .405/.81 = .50.

The consequences of not correcting for attenuation can be quite profound as the preceding example illustrates. Fan (2003) explains,

> The attenuation on sample correlation coefficients caused by measurement error may be more severe than many researchers realize. In many situations, it is not uncommon to have measurement reliabilities in the range of .60 to .80. Under such conditions, even the upper confidence interval limit itself may fail to capture the true correlation between two composites. (p. 923)

Reliabilities in the social sciences are typically rather low. Osborne (2003) found that the average reliability reported in psychology journals is .83. Lou, Abrami, Spence, Poulsen, Chambers, and d'Apollonia (1996) report a typical reliability on standardized achievement tests of .85 and a reliability of .75 for unstandardized tests of academic achievement. Within our meta-analysis, reliabilities for measures of leadership and student achievement that were reported in studies were used to correct the correlations in those studies for attenuation. When reliabilities were not reported in a study, estimates based on the observed distribution of reliabilities were used (see Hunter & Schmidt, 1990).

It should be noted that corrections for other artifacts would have increased our estimation of the true relationship or "construct level" (Hunter & Schmidt, 2004, p. 31) relationship between district achievement and student achievement. For example, Hunter and Schmidt (2004) note that virtually every study is susceptible to deviations from perfect construct validity in the independent and dependent variables. Had these artifacts been included in our corrections, the reported correlation between district leadership and student achievement would have been greater than .24.

Finally, it should be noted that Baugh (2002) cautions against the overuse of correction techniques. He states, "Correction of effect sizes for unreliability of scores has obvious benefits and yet requires considerable caution—the correction itself can yield an adjusted effect size correlation greater than 1.00 . . . Attenuation adjustments to effect sizes are not the norm; therefore, presentation of both adjusted and unadjusted estimates allows ready comparisons of effect sizes across studies" (p. 260).

In light of Baugh's caution, it is important to report our findings with and without the artifact corrections. The overall correlation between district leadership and student achievement reported in chapter 1 is .24. This correlation was computed using data from fourteen different reports (involving 1,210 districts) and is based on a random effects model (as opposed to a fixed effects model). Also it excludes two outlier findings. Correlations from each report were extracted when directly reported or computed (or imputed) when correlations were not reported. Procedures used to compute or impute correlations followed the same protocols as those described in Marzano, Waters, and McNulty (2005, Technical Note 4, pp. 133–147).

The computed and imputed correlations used to derive the .24 average were corrected for attenuation because of error of measurement in the dependent and independent variables and were weighted by sample size. Table TN1.2-1 reports other weighted average correlations computed under different sets of assumptions such as outliers being included as opposed to excluded, fixed versus random effects models, and correcting for attenuation versus not correcting for attenuation. Confidence intervals for corrected correlations were adjusted using the procedures described by Lipsey and Wilson (2001, pp. 109–110).

Table TN1.2-1 Weighted Correlations Between District Leadership and Student Achievement Under Different Sets of Assumptions

	Number of Reports (Districts)	Fixed Effects Model	Random Effects Model
Corrected for attenuation			
Outliers included	16 (1,427)	.188	.195
Outliers excluded	14 (1,210)	.243	.243
Not corrected for attenuation			
Outliers included	16 (1,427)	.148	.151
Outliers excluded	14 (1,210)	.191	.191

Note: All correlations are significant ($p < .05$).

As indicated in table TN1.2-1, the reported correlation in chapter 1 of .24 is the largest in the set. One might consider it the "best case finding" from the set along with its resulting predictive interpretation that a one standard deviation increase in district leadership is associated with a 9.5 percentile point increase in average student achievement across the district (assuming that average district achievement began at the 50th percentile). The interpretation for the lowest correlation in the set (r = .148) would be that a one standard deviation increase in district leadership is associated with a 6 percentile point increase in average student achievement across the district.

In an attempt to understand the factors affecting our reported average correlation of .24, we also examined the influence of a number of moderator variables. Specifically, we examined seven moderator variables for their relationship with the effect sizes (that is, correlation sizes) computed in our meta-analysis using the fixed effects analysis of variance techniques described by Hedges and Olkin (1985).

(1) *Reliability of dependent measure*: Reliability of the dependent measure refers to the reliability of measure of student achievement in the studies. Each reported or imputed reliability was categorized as high, medium, or low using the following criteria:

  High: .80 or above

  Medium: .65 to .79

  Low: Below .65

Table TN1.2-2 presents the findings for this analysis.

Table TN1.2-2 Reliability of Dependent Measure as Moderator Variable (Outliers Included)

Source	Point Estimation (Correlation)	95% Confidence Interval	p Value	Number of Reports
Within classes			>.05	
Between classes			.26	
High	.21	.17 to .27		15
Medium	.07	−.18 to .31		1
Low	NA	NA	NA	NA

As indicated in table TN1.2-2, there were no studies rated low regarding the reliability of the dependent measure, and only one was rated medium. The test for heterogeneity within classes was significant at the .05 level indicating that corrected correlations (point estimates) were different enough within classes (in this case, within the class of studies rated high) to reject the hypothesis that they came from the same population. However, the test of heterogeneity between classes was not significant ($p < .05$).

This might have been a function of the fact that the medium class contained only one study.

(2) *Reliability of independent measure*: Reliability of the independent measure refers to the reliability of the measure used to address district leadership. Each reported or imputed reliability was categorized as high, medium, or low using the following criteria:

> *High*:   .80 or above
>
> *Medium*:   .65 to .79
>
> *Low*:   Below .65

Table TN1.2-3 presents the findings for this analysis.

Table TN1.2-3 Reliability of Independent Measure as Moderator Variable (Outliers Included)

Source	Point Estimation (Correlation)	95% Confidence Interval	p Value	Number of Reports
Within classes			.31	
Between classes			>.01	
High	.32	.20 to .42		6
Medium	.22	.15 to .29		2
Low	.06	–.06 to .17		8

The test for heterogeneity within classes was not significant at the .05 level indicating that corrected correlations (point estimates) were not different enough within classes to reject the hypothesis that they came from the same population. However, the test of heterogeneity between classes was significant ($p < .05$). Taken at face value, these findings might indicate that studies with higher reliabilities had larger correlations.

(3) *Imputed effect size*: Imputed effect size refers to the extent to which the effect size could be directly computed versus imputed. Each effect was classified as high, medium, or low for this moderator variable using the following criteria:

> *Low*: Effect size was reported in the study or could be computed using data directly reported in the study.
>
> *Medium*: Effect size was computed using data not directly in the study but applied to the conditions of the study (such as using population standard deviations for measures used in the study).
>
> *High*: Effect size was computed using a transformation of data to approximate a Pearson correlation (such as transforming a contingency table into

an estimate of a Pearson correlation while assuming specific distribution characteristics even though they were not reported in the study).

Table TN1.2-4 presents the findings for this analysis.

Table TN1.2-4 Imputed Effect Size (Outliers Included)

Source	Point Estimation (Correlation)	95% Confidence Interval	p Value	Number of Reports
Within classes			>.04	
Between classes			.47	
Low	.30	.04 to .52		2
Medium	NA	NA		
High	.20	.15 to .26		14

Table TN1.2-4 indicates that there were no studies classified as medium for this moderator variable. The test for heterogeneity within classes was significant at the .05 level indicating that corrected correlations (point estimates) were different enough within classes to reject the hypothesis that they came from the same population. However, the test of heterogeneity between classes was not significant ($p < .05$).

(4) *Quality of dependent measure*: Quality of dependent measure refers to the extent to which the dependent measure was a direct measure of student achievement. Each effect was classified as high, medium, or low for this moderator variable using the following criteria:

> *High*: Dependent measure reported student achievement using aggregate scores from some continuous measure of achievement (such as aggregate normal curve equivalence scores from a state or standardized test).

> *Medium*: Dependent measure reported student achievement using aggregate scores that were transformations of some continuous measure of achievement (such as percentage of students above a given criterion score on a state or standardized test).

> *Low*: Dependent measure employed some type of composite index purported to measure achievement.

Table TN1.2-5 (page 124) presents the findings for this analysis.

Table TN1.2-5 Quality of Dependent Measure (Outliers Included)

Source	Point Estimation (Correlation)	95% Confidence Interval	p Value	Number of Reports
Within classes			.66	
Between classes			>.01	
High	.29	.20 to .37		7
Medium	.21	.14 to .29		6
Low	−.05	−.20 to .10		3

The test for heterogeneity within classes was not significant at the .05 level indicating that corrected correlations (point estimates) were not different enough within classes to reject the hypothesis that they came from the same population. However, the test of heterogeneity between classes was significant ($p < .01$). At face value, one might conclude that quality of the dependent measure is related to effect size. Specifically, the point estimation for studies rated low is substantially lower than the point estimation for studies rated medium and high.

(5) *Quality of independent measure*: Quality of independent measure refers to the extent to which the independent measure was a direct measure of district leadership. Each effect was classified as high, medium, or low for this moderator variable using the following criteria:

High: Independent measure directly addressed district leadership.

Medium: Independent measure addressed aggregated variables that were considered defining characteristics of district leadership.

Low: Independent measure was based on assumptions regarding the relationship between district factors and student achievement.

Table TN1.2-6 presents the findings for this analysis.

The test for heterogeneity within classes was significant at the .05 level indicating that corrected correlations (point estimates) were different enough within classes to reject the hypothesis that they came from the same population. However, the test of heterogeneity between classes was not significant ($p < .05$).

Table TN1.2-6 Quality of Independent Measure (Outliers Included)

Source	Point Estimation (Correlation)	95% Confidence Interval	p Value	Number of Reports
Within classes			>.05	
Between classes			.24	
High	.28	.16 to .39		4
Medium	.16	.08 to .24		7
Low	.27	.14 to .31		5

(6) *Date of publication*: Date of publication refers to the time at which studies were made available to the public. Studies were organized into four categories relative to this variable: 1970s, 1980s, 1990s, and 2000s.

Table TN1.2-7 presents the findings for this analysis.

Table TN1.2-7 Date of Publication (Outliers Included)

Source	Point Estimation (Correlation)	95% Confidence Interval	p Value	Number of Reports
Within classes			.052	
Between classes			.22	
1970s	.26	.09 to .41		2
1980s	.27	.17 to .37		4
1990s	.27	.08 to .43		4
2000s	.16	.09 to .23		6

The test for heterogeneity within classes was not significant at the .05 level indicating that corrected correlations (point estimates) were not different enough within classes to reject the hypothesis that they came from the same population. Similarly, the test of heterogeneity between classes was also not significant ($p < .05$). Taken at face value, one might conclude that there is no difference in the effect sizes from decade to decade.

(7) *Publication type*: Publication type refers to the venue in which the studies were made available to the public. Each effect study was classified into one of three categories: dissertations, journals, or reports.

Table TN1.2-8 (page 126) presents the findings for this analysis.

Table TN1.2-8 Publication Type (Outliers Included)

Source	Point Estimation (Correlation)	95% Confidence Interval	p Value	Number of Reports
Within classes			>.05	
Between classes			.22	
Dissertations	.19	.13 to .25		11
Journals	.28	.16 to .39		3
Reports	.38	-.07 to .71		2

The test for heterogeneity within classes was significant at the .05 level indicating that corrected correlations (point estimates) were different enough within classes to reject the hypothesis that they came from the same population. However, the test of heterogeneity between classes was not significant ($p < .05$).

Technical Note 1.3: Binomial Effect Size Display Interpretation of Correlations

Another interpretation of the correlation of .24 for district leadership is presented in table TN1.3-1.

Table TN1.3-1 Interpretation of a Correlation of .24 in Terms of Expected Passing Rates for Districts

	Percentage of Districts Passing the Test (%)	Percentage of Districts Failing the Test (%)
Districts in top half of leadership	62	38
Districts in bottom half of leadership	38	62

The rows in table TN1.3-1 are titled *districts in top half of leadership* and *districts in bottom half of leadership,* respectively. To interpret this, assume that all the districts in the United States were ordered in terms of their leadership on some continuous scale. It is reasonable to assume that they would form a normal distribution like that depicted in figure TN1.3-1.

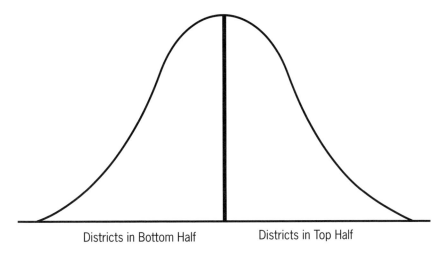

Districts in Bottom Half   Districts in Top Half

Figure TN1.3-1 Distribution of districts ordered by leadership

The top half of the distribution in figure TN1.3-1 contains the top 50% of districts in terms of their leadership; the bottom half of the distribution contains the bottom 50% of districts.

To interpret the correlation of .24 depicted in table TN1.3-1, one assumes that a test is given to all the students in all the districts in the United States. For a district to pass the test, the average score for the students in the district must surpass a certain "cut score." Additionally, the test is designed in such a way that the general expectation is that 50% of districts will pass the test and 50% of districts will fail the test. Table TN1.3-1 demonstrates how the expected passing rate changes based on whether a district is in the top half of the distribution in terms of leadership or in the bottom half of the distribution. As table TN1.3-1 indicates, in those districts in the top half of the leadership distribution, 62% of the districts would be expected to pass the test and 38% would be expected to fail the test. For those districts in the bottom half of the leadership distribution, the expectation is the opposite. Only 38% of the districts would pass the test and 62% would fail the test. Stated differently, the districts in the top half of the leadership distribution would have a 24% higher passing rate.

This interpretation is derived from the binomial effect size display (BESD). As described by Rosenthal and Rubin (1982), to employ the BESD, the predictor variable is thought of as being dichotomized into two distinct groups. One group might be the experimental group; the other might be the control group. Similarly, one group might be high performers on some variable (such as district leadership); the other might be low performers on the same variable. In the BESD illustration used in table TN1.3-1, the dichotomized independent variable is district leadership. Similarly, when employing the BESD, the predicted variable is dichotomized into success or failure on some criterion measure. In this case, that criterion measure is average district achievement on a test.

A common convention employed with the BESD is to assume that the expectation for the predicted variable is a success rate of 0.50. To compute the BESD, the correlation coefficient is divided by 2 and then added to and subtracted from the baseline expected success rate or 0.50. For example, if the r between predictor and predicted is .24, then .24 ÷ 2 = 0.12. The percentage of subjects (districts) in the higher-performing group (that is, the top half of the leadership distribution) that would be expected to "succeed" on the predicted variable is computed as 0.50 + 0.12 = 0.62. The percentage of subjects (districts) in the lower-performing group (the bottom half of the leadership distribution) that would be expected to "fail" on the criterion measure is 0.50 – 0.12 = 0.38. The converse of these computations is used for the low-performing group. Rosenthal and Rubin (1982) make the case for the use of BESD as a realistic and useful representation of the size of the treatment effect when the outcome variable is continuous, provided that the groups are of equal size and variance.

Cohen (1988) dramatically illustrates the use of the BESD using an example from medicine. This is depicted in table TN1.3-2.

Table TN1.3-2 Binomial Effect Size Display With 1% of Variance (r = .10)

Accounted for by Hypothetical Medical Treatment			
Group	Outcome %		
	% Alive	% Dead	Total
Treatment	55	45	100
Control	45	55	100

Note: Constructed from data in Cohen (1988); r stands for the Pearson product–moment correlation coefficient.

Table TN1.3-2 exemplifies a situation in which the independent variable (such as membership in the experimental or control group) accounts for only 1% of the variance in the dependent variable (that is, r = .10). The assumption here is that the independent variable is some sort of medical treatment that accounts for 1% of the variance in the outcome measure, which is being alive or dead. Yet this 1% of explained variance translates into a 10 percentage point difference in terms of patients who are alive (or dead) based on group membership. As Cohen (1988) notes,

> This means, for example, that a difference in percent alive between 45 and 55, which most people would consider important (*alive*, mind you!) yields r = .10, and "only 1% of the variance accounted for," an amount that operationally defines a "small" effect in my scheme. . . . "Death" tends to concentrate the mind. But this in turn reinforces the principle that the size of an effect can only be appraised in the context of the substantive issues involved. An r^2 of .01 is indeed small in absolute terms, but when it represents a ten percentage point increase in survival, it may well be considered large. (p. 534)

This same point is further dramatized by Abelson (1985). After analyzing the effect of various physical skills on the batting averages of professional baseball players, he found that the percentage of variance accounted for by these skills was a minuscule 0.00317—not quite one-third of 1% ($r = .056$). Commenting on the implications for interpreting education research, Abelson notes,

> One should not necessarily be scornful of minuscule values for percentage of variance explained, provided there is statistical assurance that these values are significantly above zero, and that the degree of potential cumulation is substantial. (p. 133)

Finally, Cohen (1988) exhorts, "The next time you read 'only X% of the variance is accounted for,' remember Abelson's paradox" (p. 535).

Technical Note 1.4: Correlation for Five District Responsibilities or Initiatives

Tables TN1.4-1 through TN1.4-5 (pages 130–131) report weighted average correlations computed under different sets of assumptions (that is, outliers included as opposed to excluded, fixed-effects versus random-effects models, and correcting for attenuation versus not correcting for attenuation) for the following variables: (1) ensuring collaborative goal setting, (2) establishing nonnegotiable goals for achievement and instruction, (3) creating board alignment with and support of district goals, (4) monitoring achievement and instruction goals, and (5) allocating resources to support goals for achievement and instruction.

Table TN1.4-1 Ensuring Collaborative Goal Setting

	Number of Reports (Districts)	Fixed Effects Model	Random Effects Model
Corrected for attenuation			
Outliers included	9 (1,363)	.170	.275
Outliers excluded	7 (702)	.238	.238
Not corrected for attenuation			
Outliers included	9 (1,363)	.128	.196
Outliers excluded	7 (702)	.202	.213

Note: All correlations are significant ($p < .05$).

Table TN1.4-2 Establishing Nonnegotiable Goals for Achievement and Instruction

Number of Reports (Districts)	Fixed Effects Model	Random Effects Model
Corrected for attenuation		
8 (728)	.327	.350
Not corrected for attenuation		
8 (728)	.254	.267

Note: All correlations are significant ($p < .05$). There were no outlier data points.

Table TN1.4-3 Creating Board Alignment With and Support of District Goals

Number of Reports (Districts)	Fixed Effects Model	Random Effects Model
Corrected for attenuation		
5 (324)	.289	.289
Not corrected for attenuation		
5 (324)	.238	.238

Note: All correlations are significant ($p < .05$). There were no outlier data points.

Table TN1.4-4 Monitoring Achievement and Instruction Goals

	Number of Reports (Districts)	Fixed Effects Model	Random Effects Model
Corrected for attenuation			
Outliers included	9 (691)	.290	.327
Outliers excluded	7 (612)	.272	.284
Not corrected for attenuation			
Outliers included	9 (691)	.222	.246
Outliers excluded	7 (612)	.233	.259

Note: All correlations are significant ($p < .05$).

Table TN1.4-5 Allocating Resources to Support the Goals for Achievement and Instruction

Number of Reports (Districts)	Fixed Effects Model	Random Effects Model
Corrected for attenuation		
6 (482)	.259	.276
Not corrected for attenuation		
6 (482)	.223	.237

Note: All correlations are significant ($p < .05$). There were no outlier data points.

Technical Note 1.5: Correlation for *Defined Autonomy*

Two studies representing 198 districts included correlations for site-based management. Table TN1.5-1 reports weighted average correlations computed under different sets of assumptions (such as fixed-effects versus random-effects models and correcting for attenuation versus not correcting for attenuation).

Table TN1.5-1 Site-Based Management

Number of Reports (Districts)	Fixed Effects Model	Random Effects Model
Corrected for attenuation		
2 (198)	−.103	−.014
Not corrected for attenuation		
2 (198)	−.08	−.026

Note: No correlations are significant ($p < .05$).

One study (Byrd, 2001) involving 163 districts reported a correlation of .28 (corrected random effects) for "campus autonomy;" however, the study was very vague in terms of its description of the characteristics of autonomy. The study also reported a correlation of –.16 (corrected random effects model) for site-based management. The weighted average correlations for campus autonomy under various interpretational models are presented in table TN1.5-2.

Table TN1.5-2 Campus Autonomy

Number of Reports (Districts)	Fixed Effects Model	Random Effects Model
Corrected for attenuation		
1 (163)	.28	.28
Not corrected for attenuation		
1 (163)	.22	.22

Note: All correlations are significant ($p < .05$).

Technical Note 1.6: Tenure

Table TN1.6 reports weighted average correlations for tenure under different sets of assumptions (such as fixed-effects versus random-effects models and correcting for attenuation versus not correcting for attenuation).

Table TN1.6 Tenure

Number of Reports (Districts)	Fixed Effects Model	Random Effects Model
Corrected for attenuation		
2 (205)	.191	.191
Not corrected for attenuation		
2 (265)	.160	.160

Note: All correlations are significant ($p < .05$).

Technical Note 1.7: District, School, and Teacher Effects

A hierarchical linear model was used to compute the estimated effects of districts, schools, and teachers reported in tables 1.1 and 1.2. Data were drawn from the study by Nye, Konstantopoulos, and Hedges (2004). That study, commonly referred to as the Tennessee Class Size Experiment or Project STAR (student–teacher achievement ratio; for details, see Nye et al., 2004), involved seventy-nine elementary schools in forty-two districts in Tennessee. At kindergarten, students were randomly assigned to classrooms in one of three conditions: (1) small classes, (2) larger classes, or (3) larger classes with a full-time aide. Teachers were also randomly assigned to classes of different types. Random assignment was maintained through the third grade.

Since the classes within each school are initially equivalent (due to random assignment) any systematic differences in achievement among classes must be due to one of two reasons: the treatment [class size] or differences in teacher effectiveness. (p. 241)

To estimate the effects of teachers and schools, Nye and colleagues (2004) used a three-level hierarchic model. The Level 1 equation contained a class-level intercept and fixed effects for previous achievement (as measured by a pretest), gender, socioeconomic status, and minority status. It also contained a residual component for the unique effect of students within classes. This constituted the within classroom variance component.

The Level 2 equation modeled the class-level intercept. It contained a school-level intercept, a fixed effect for class size, and the presence of a class aide. It also contained a residual component for the unique effect of classes within schools. This constituted the between-classes variance component.

The Level 3 equation modeled the school-level intercept. It contained an overall intercept and a residual component for the unique effect of schools. This constituted the between-school variance component.

Using the three variance components from the three levels—within classes, between classes, and between schools—various estimates of student achievement gain can be constructed. As it relates to the between-classes variance component, Nye and colleagues (2004) note,

> If teacher effects are normally distributed, these findings would suggest that the difference in achievement gains between having a 25th percentile teacher (a not so effective teacher) and a 75th percentile teacher (an effective teacher) is over one third of a standard deviation (0.35) in reading and almost half a standard deviation (0.48) in mathematics. Similarly, the difference in achievement gains between having a 50th percentile teacher (an average teacher) and a 90th percentile teacher (a very effective teacher) is about one third of a standard deviation (0.33) in reading and somewhat smaller than a half a standard deviation (0.46) in mathematics. (p. 253)

Their conclusions are based on estimating the overall between-classes variance component across grades 1 through 3. They explain,

> The teacher effect variance on reading achievement gains rounds to [alpha squared] = 0.07 in every grade which implies a teacher effect standard deviation of [sigma] = 0.26. The difference between the 25th and 75th percentiles of the standard normal distribution is 1.34 standard deviations, so the difference in class mean reading achievement

between a 25th percentile and 75th percentile teacher is (1.34) (0.26) = 0.35. The other calculations were analogous. (p. 255)

In effect, Nye and colleagues estimated the aggregate between-classes variance component for reading across grades 1, 2, and 3 by noting that all three variance components rounded to .07. Specifically, they report in table 5 (page 246) those components are .066, .068, and .074, respectively. Thus, the estimated aggregated standard deviation is $.07^{.5}$ or .26. With an estimate of the aggregate between-class standard deviation, predictions can be made for a student with average achievement within a particular class. This is documented in the preceding quotation from page 253 in which the difference in expected achievement between students with a 25th percentile teacher and a 75th percentile teacher is computed. In general, then, one simply selects two points of reference (such as 25th and 75th percentiles) in terms of status regarding the teacher effect (that is, the between-class standard deviations) and then computes the predicted status on achievement.

Although Nye and colleagues did not choose to do so, the same logic can be applied to the between-school variance component. One begins with an estimate of the aggregate variance component across grades 1, 2, and 3. As reported by Nye and colleagues (2004, table 5), the between-school variance components for first, second, and third grades are .097, .026, and .019, respectively with a mean of .047. Since the first grade variance component of .097 is much larger than the others, we used a conservative estimate of .03, which is equivalent to the rounded value of the median. Consequently, the estimated aggregate standard deviation for reading is $.03^{.5}$ or .17. Using the same logic as that applied to the teacher effect (the between-classes variance component), one might say that predicted difference in achievement between a student in a 50th percentile school and a student in an 84th percentile school (a school one standard deviation above the mean) is .17 standard deviations or about 7 percentile points. Similarly, the predicted difference in student achievement between a student in a 50th percentile school and a student in a 98th percentile school (a school two standard deviations above the mean) is .34 standard deviations or about 13 percentile points. Using these estimates, one can contrast the expected difference in achievement between students whose teachers have different levels of competence and whose schools have different levels of competence. This is done in table TN1.7-1 for reading and table TN1.7-2 for mathematics.

Table TN1.7-1 Reading

Teacher	School	Predicted *SDs* Above Mean in Achievement	Predicted Percentile Gain From 50th Percentile	Final Predicted Percentile Rank
One *SD* above mean	At mean	.26	10	60th
Two *SDs* above mean	At mean	.52	20	70th
At mean	One *SD* above mean	.17	7	57th
At mean	Two *SDs* above mean	.34	13	63rd

Table TN1.7-2 Mathematics

Teacher	School	Predicted *SDs* Above Mean in Achievement	Predicted Percentile Gain From 50th Percentile	Final Predicted Percentile Rank
One *SD* above mean	At mean	.36	14	64th
Two *SDs* above mean	At mean	.72	26	76th
At mean	One *SD* above mean	.22	9	59th
At mean	Two *SDs* above mean	.44	17	67th

The first two rows of table TN1.7-1 (reading) simply report the results described by Nye and colleagues (2004) using different reference points. To illustrate, consider the results for reading. A 50th percentile student in the classroom of a teacher with one standard deviation above the mean in terms of pedagogical competence would be expected to increase his or her achievement by .26 standard deviations or 10 percentile points. A 50th percentile student in the classroom of a teacher with two standard deviations above the mean in terms of pedagogical competence would be expected to increase his or her achievement by .52 standard deviations or 20 percentile points. In both cases, the school is assumed to be at the 50th percentile in terms of its effectiveness. The last two rows of table TN1.7-1 hold the teacher at the 50th percentile but increase the school's effectiveness at enhancing student achievement by one standard deviation and two standard deviations, respectively. Given this enhanced effectiveness at the school level, a 50th percentile student in a school one standard deviation above the mean would be expected to exhibit a 7 percentile point increase in achievement, and a 50th percentile student in a school two standard deviations above the mean would be expected to exhibit a 13 percentile point increase. The same logic and interpretation apply to the results in mathematics depicted in table TN1.7-2.

The preceding discussion applies to effects of teachers and schools. To include an estimate of the effect of districts, we partitioned the school effect as reported by Nye and colleagues (2004) into school and district components. To do so, we used the findings reported by Alexander (1976). Using grade 3, 5, 7, and 9 achievement data in vocabulary, reading, and mathematics from twenty-four districts, Alexander estimated that between 47% and 64% of the variance in achievement between schools is attributable to district differences:

> From 47 to 64 percent of the between-school variance in the three achievement tests also lies between districts. Although we have no direct data on the total achievement variance lying between Maryland schools, we might assume, based on the findings of Hauser (1972), Coleman et al. (1966) and others, that this would be on the order of 10-20 percent. If so, then roughly 5 to 10 percent of the total variance in student achievement outcomes lies between school districts in these data. It is this variance which is analyzed in our district-level achievement model. (Alexander, 1976, p. 147)

Using these findings as the basis for our inferences, we conservatively ascribed 40% (as opposed to 47%) of the variance between schools in the Nye et al. study to district factors. Specifically, we split the school-level standard deviations reported above 60/40 for schools and districts, respectively. This allowed for the district estimates reported in the following tables TN1.7-3 and TN1.7-4.

Table TN1.7-3 Effect of Districts in Reading Achievement

Teacher	School	District	Predicted *SDs* Above Mean in Achievement	Predicted Percentile Gain From 50th Percentile	Final Predicted Percentile Rank
At mean	At mean	One *SD* above mean	.07 (.17 × .40)	3	53rd
At mean	At mean	Two *SDs* above mean	.14 (.34 × .40)	6	56th

Table TN1.7-4 Effects of Districts in Mathematics Achievement

Teacher	School	District	Predicted SDs Above Mean in Achievement	Predicted Percentile Gain From 50th Percentile	Final Predicted Percentile Rank
At mean	At mean	One SD above mean	.09 (.22 × .40)	4	54th
At mean	At mean	Two SDs above mean	.18 (.44 × .40)	7	57th

Table TN1.7-3 demonstrates that an increase in district effectiveness of one standard deviation (keeping the teacher and school at the 50th percentile) would be associated with an increase of 3 percentile points in reading achievement; an increase in district effectiveness of two standard deviations would be associated with an increase of 6 percentile points in reading. Table TN1.7-4 presents the results of similar calculations for mathematics.

When the partitioned effects of districts and schools are combined again, one obtains the predictions in tables TN1.7-5 and TN1.7-6 (page 138).

Table TN1.7-5 Effects of Districts and Schools Combined in Reading

Teacher	School	Predicted SDs Above Mean in Achievement Because of School	District	Predicted SDs Above Mean in Achievement Because of District	Combined Predicted Percentile Gain From 50th Percentile	Final Predicted Percentile Rank
At mean	One SD Above Mean	.10 (.17 × .60)	One SD above mean	.07 (.17 × .40)	7	57th
At mean	At mean	.20 (.34 × .60)	Two SDs above mean	.14 (.34 × .40)	13	63rd

Table TN1.7-6 Effects of Districts and Schools Combined in Mathematics

Teacher	School	Predicted SDs Above Mean in Achievement Because of School	District	Predicted SDs Above Mean in Achievement Because of District	Combined Predicted Percentile Gain From 50th Percentile	Final Predicted Percentile Rank
At mean	One SD above mean	.13 (.22 × .60)	One SD above mean	.09 (.22 × .40)	9	59th
At mean	At mean	.26 (.44 × .60)	Two SDs above mean	.18 (.44 ×.40)	17	67th

The first thing to note about tables TN1.7-5 and TN1.7-6 is that combined estimates of achievement gain are the same as reported in tables TN1.7-1 and TN1.7-2 for the school effect taken from the Nye et al. (2004) study. This is necessarily so because the school effect from that study was partitioned to generate the estimate of the separate effects for schools and districts. This also provides a rationale for our partitioning of the standard deviation as opposed to the variance component. Traditionally, one partitions the variance component as opposed to the standard deviation. However, in this case, such a practice would produce a combined effect for the school and district greater than the initial estimate of the school effect. To illustrate, consider the .03 between-school variance component for reading and its associated standard deviation of .17. Again, we ascribed 60% of the standard deviation or .10 to schools and 40% or .07 to districts. Thus, the combined effect of district and school is equal to the original school effect in standard deviation units (0.10 + 0.07 = 0.17). Partitioning the variance component would have resulted in a very different and counterintuitive result. Specifically, the variance component for school was 0.03. Sixty percent of this is 0.018, which translates to a standard deviation of 0.13. Forty percent of .03 is .012, which translates to a standard deviation of .11. In this scenario, the combined effect of the schools and districts when translated back to standard deviation units would be .24 (0.13 + 0.11 = 0.24), which is larger than the original effect of schools in standard deviation units.

Technical Note 3.1: Standardized Mean Difference Effect Size (ESd)

A commonly used index of association is the standardized mean difference. Commonly referred to as an *effect size,* the index is the difference between experimental and control means divided by an estimate of the population standard deviation—hence, the name, standardized mean difference or ES*d*.

$$ESd = \frac{\text{experimental group mean} - \text{control group mean}}{\text{estimate of population standard deviation}}$$

Theorists have suggested a variety of ways to estimate the population standard deviation along with techniques for computing the effect size index under different assumptions (see Cohen, 1988; Glass, 1976; Hedges & Olkin, 1985). The effect size index used in many studies employs the pooled standard deviation from experimental and control groups as the population estimate. It is frequently referred to as Cohen's d. It will be referred to here as ESd.

To illustrate the use of ESd, assume that the achievement mean of a school with a given characteristic is 90 on a standardized test and that the mean of a school that does not possess this characteristic is 80. Also assume that the population standard deviation is 10. The ESd would be the following:

$$ESd = \frac{90 - 80}{10} = 1.0$$

This ESd can be interpreted in the following way: the mean of the experimental group is 1.0 standard deviation larger than the mean of the control group. One might infer, then, that the characteristic possessed by the experimental school raises achievement test scores by one standard deviation. Thus, the effect size (ESd) expresses the differences between means in standardized or Z score form. It is this characteristic that gives rise to an interpretation in terms of percentile gain.

Technical Note 3.2: Interpretation of Durlak and Weissberg (2007) Findings

Durlak and Weissberg (2007) report an ESd of .31. The interpretation presented in chapter 3 is based on Cohen's U3 (Cohen, 1988). Basically, if one assumes that 50% of students in the control group pass a particular test, U3 indicates the percentage of students one would expect to pass in the experimental group. Lipsey and Wilson (2001, p. 153) provide conversion charts to translate an ESd to an estimate of passing rate in the experimental group under the assumption that the passing rate in the control group is 50%.

Appendix

Reports Used in Meta-Analysis

Adams, J. P. (1987). Superintendents and effective schools. *Dissertation Abstracts International, 48*(09), 2199A. (UMI No. 8727818)

Alexander, G. (1976). School district effects on academic achievement. *American Sociological Review, 41,* 144–151.

Allen, R. W. (1996). A comparison of school effectiveness and school achievement for schools in Arkansas. *Dissertation Abstracts International, 57*(07), 2749A. (UMI No. 9700324)

Bell, L. A. (1996). School-based management and student achievement. *Dissertation Abstract International, 57*(09), 3755A. (UMI No. 9701364)

Bidwell, K. (1975). School district organization and student achievement. *American Sociological Review, 40,* 55–70.

Brock, J. H. (1986). A study of the relationship of pupil achievement test scores in reading and mathematics to pupil expenditures and selected district socioeconomic variables. *Dissertation Abstracts International, 48*(04), 831A. (UMI No. 8715918)

Burnett, R. D. (1989). The effects of superintendents' leadership behaviors in curriculum and instruction upon student achievement in South Carolina public school districts. *Dissertation Abstracts International, 50*(06), 1494A. (UMI No. 8921454)

Byrd, J. K. (2001). Effective superintendent leadership strategies and management techniques for improving student performance as perceived by superintendents in selected school districts in Texas. *Dissertation Abstracts International, 62*(07), 2294A. (UMI No. 3020012)

Clore, W. P. (1991). The relationship of superintendent instructional leadership behavior and school district demographics to student achievement. *Dissertation Abstracts International, 52*(04), 1142A. (UMI No. 9128196)

Coladarci, T., Smith, L., & Whiteley, G. (2005). *The re-inventing schools implementation monitoring survey, Alaska benchmark/high school graduation qualifying examination data and relationship between the two.* Anchorage, AK: Re-Inventing Schools Coalition.

Cotter, M. (2001). Strategic leadership for student achievement: An exploratory analysis of school board-superintendent governance and development practices. *Dissertation Abstracts International, 62*(06), 1993A. (UMI No. 3017528)

Duvall, S. A. (2005). *Superintendent evaluation and other influences on the school board and superintendent relationship: Measuring strength of relationship.* Unpublished doctoral dissertation, Eastern Michigan University.

Endeman, J. L. (1990). Visionary leadership in superintendents and its effect on organizational out-comes. *Dissertation Abstracts International, 52*(05), 1589A. (UMI No. 9128127)

Goodman, R. H., Fullbright, L., & Zimmerman, W. G. (1997). *Getting there from here: School board-superintendent collaboration—Creating a school governance team capable of raising student achievement.* Alexandria, VA: Educational Research Service.

Hart, A. W. (1983). An exploration of the effects of superintendents on the instructional performance of school districts. *Dissertation Abstracts International, 44*(12), 3556A. (UMI No. 8405914)

Hart, A. W., & Ogawa, R. T. (1987). The influence of superintendents on the academic achievement of school districts. *Journal of Educational Administration, 25*(1), 72–84.

Hoyle, J., Hogan, D., Skrla, L., & Ealy, C. (2001). Superintendent performance evaluation and its relationships to district student performance. *21st Century Challenges for School Administrators: NCPEA Yearbook, 7*, 272–285.

Jackson, R. M. (1991). The superintendent and school improvement: Antecedents, actions and out-comes. *Dissertation Abstracts International, 52*(11), 3784A. (UMI No. 9210063)

Johnson, K. (1997). The relationship of superintendent tenure to school performance in Arkansas. *Dissertation Abstracts International, 58*(08), 2928A. (UMI No. 9805852)

Mocek, R. C. (2002). The influence of educational administrators' leadership behaviors on student achievement in reading. *Dissertation Abstracts International, 63*(06), 2069A. (UMI No. 3055455)

Morgan, G. W. (1990). School district effectiveness and the leadership of the superintendent of schools. *Dissertation Abstracts International, 51*(07), 2223A. (UMI No. 9033609)

Muller, R. W. (1989). Instructional leadership superintendents' competencies related to student achievement. *Dissertation Abstracts International, 50*(09), 2737A. (UMI No. 8920786)

Sanchez, A. P. (2003). The relationship between the superintendent's perceptions of the utiliza-tion of technology to increase student achievement and actual district student achievement. *Dissertation Abstracts International, 64*(07), 2460A. (UMI No. 3099261)

Vaughan, N. K. (2002). The relationship between student performance and the leadership behavior of superintendents in Texas public school districts. *Dissertation Abstracts International, 63*(06), 2080A. (UMI No. 3058161)

Veltri, P. J. (2001). The relationship between school districts' planning practices, student achieve-ment, and the implementation of the correlates of effective schools. *Dissertation Abstracts International, 62*(04), 1294A. (UMI No. 3010890)

Wallace, M. G. (1998). Student performance and administrative interventions within the successful schools consortium. *Dissertation Abstracts International, 59*(07), 2291A. (UMI No. 9838753)

Wodderson-Perez, M. (2000). The relationship of superintendent leadership styles to student achieve-ment and school district financial and demographic factors in Texas. *Dissertation Abstracts International, 61*(8), 3020A. (UMI No. 9982149)

References

Abelson, R. P. (1985). A variance explained paradox: When a little is a lot. *Psychological Bulletin, 97*, 166–169.

Abrams, L. M. (2007). Implications of high stakes testing for the use of formative classroom assessment. In J. H. McMillan (Ed.), *Formative classroom assessment: Theory into practice* (pp. 79–98). New York: Teachers College Press.

Ainsworth, L., & Viegut, D. (2006). *Common formative assessments.* Thousand Oaks, CA: Corwin Press.

Andrews, J. W., Blackmon, C. R., & Mackey, J. A. (1980). Preservice performance and the national teacher examinations. *Phi Delta Kappan, 61*(5), 358–359.

Argyris, C., & Schön, D. (1974). *Theory in practice: Increasing professional effectiveness.* San Francisco: Jossey-Bass.

Argyris, C., & Schön, D. (1978). *Organizational learning: A theory of action perspective.* Reading, MA: Addison-Wesley.

Armour-Thomas, E., Clay, C., Domanico, R., Bruno, K., & Allen, B. (1989). *An outlier study of elementary and middle schools in New York City: Final report.* New York: New York City Board of Education.

Ashton, P., & Crocker, L. (1987, May/June). Systematic study of planned variations: The essential focus of teacher education reform. *Journal of Teacher Education, 38*, 2–8.

Baker, D. P., & LeTendre, G. K. (2005). *National differences, global similarities: World culture and the future of schooling.* Stanford, CA: Stanford University Press.

Barton, P. E. (2006). Needed: Higher standards for accountability. *Educational Leadership, 64*(3), 28–31.

Baugh, F. (2002). Correcting effect sizes for score reliability: A reminder that measurement and substantive issues are linked inextricably. *Educational and Psychological Measurement, 62*(2), 254–263.

Bellamy, G. T., Crawford, L., Marshall, L. H., & Coulter, G. A. (2005). The fail-safe schools challenge: Leadership possibilities for high reliability organizations. *Educational Administration Quarterly, 41*, 383–412.

Bennett, W. J., Finn, C. E., Jr., & Cribb, T. E., Jr. (1999). *The educated child: A parent's guide from preschool through eighth grade.* New York: Free Press.

Berliner, D. C. (1986). In pursuit of the expert pedagogue. *Educational Researcher, 15*(7), 5–13.

Black, P., & Wiliam, D. (1998). Assessment and classroom learning. *Assessment in Education: Principles, Policy & Practice, 5*(1), 7–75.

Board of Education of the City of New York. (1987/1988). *A summary for the comprehensive school improvement and planning process.* New York: Author.

Borman, G. D., Hewes, G. M., Overman, L. T., & Brown, S. (2003). Comprehensive school reform and achievement: A meta-analysis. *Review of Educational Research, 73*(2), 125–230.

Bridges, W. (1980). *Transitions: Making sense of life's changes.* Reading, MA: Addison-Wesley.

Brown, C. A., Smith, M. S., & Stein, M. K. (1995, April). *Linking teacher support to enhanced classroom instruction.* Paper presented at the annual meeting of the American Educational Research Association, New York, NY.

Byrne, C. J. (1983). *Teacher knowledge and teacher effectiveness: A literature review, theoretical analysis and discussion of research strategy.* Paper presented at the meeting of the Northwestern Educational Research Association, Ellenville, NY.

Cambone, J., Weiss, C., & Wyeth, A. (1992). *We're not programmed for this: An exploration of the variance between the ways teachers think and the concept of shared decision making in high schools* (Occasional Paper No. 17). Cambridge, MA: National Center for Educational Leadership.

Chiseri-Strater, E., & Sunstein, B. S. (2006). *What works? A practical guide for teacher research.* Alexandria, VA: Association for Supervision and Curriculum Development.

Cizek, G. J. (2007). Formative classroom and large-scale assessment: Implications for future research and development. In J. H. McMillan (Ed.), *Formative classroom assessment: Theory into practice* (pp. 99–115). New York: Teachers College Press.

Cohen, J. (1988). Statistical power analysis for the behavioral sciences (2nd ed.). New York: Academic Press.

Cohen, J., Cohen, P., West, S. G., & Aiken, L. S. (2003). *Applied multiple regression/correlation analysis for the behavioral sciences* (3rd ed.). Mahwah, NJ: Erlbaum.

Coleman, J. S., Campbell, E. Q., Hobson, C. J., McPartland, J., Mood, A., Weinfield, F. D., et al. (1966). *Equality of educational opportunity.* Washington, DC: U.S. Government Printing Office.

Conley, D. (2003). *Who governs our schools? Changing roles and responsibilities.* New York: Teachers College Press.

Connecticut State Board of Education. (2002). *Position statement on educational leadership: A collaborative effort to improve student achievement.* Hartford, CT: Author.

Cooper, H., Charlton, K., Valentine, J. C., & Muhlenbruck, L. (2000). Making the most of summer school: A meta-analysis and narrative review. *Monographs of the Society for Research in Child Development, 65*(1, Serial No. 260), 1–118.

Cooper, H., & Hedges, L. V. (Eds.). (1994). *The handbook of research synthesis.* New York: Russell Sage.

Council for Educational Development and Research. (1997). *Where did the money go?* Washington, DC: Author.

Cuban, L. (1987, July). *Constancy and change in schools (1880s to the present).* Paper presented at the Conference on Restructuring Education, Keystone, CO.

Darling-Hammond, L. (1997). *Doing what matters most: Investing in quality teaching.* New York: National Commission on Teaching and America's Future.

Darling-Hammond, L. (2000). Teacher quality and student achievement: A review of state policy evidence. *Education Policy Analysis Archives, 8*(1), 1–50. Accessed at http://epaa.asu.edu/epaa/v8n1/ on January 24, 2009.

David, J. L. (1996). The who, what, and why of site-based management. *Educational Leadership, 53*(4), 4–9.

de Leeuw, J. (2004). Senior editor introduction. In R. A. Berk, Ed., *Regression analysis: A constructive critique* (pp. xi–xv). Thousand Oaks, CA: Sage.

Diamond, J. (2005). *Collapse: How societies choose to fail or succeed.* New York: Penguin.

Dimmock, C. (2000). *Designing the learning-centered school: A cross-cultural perspective.* London: Falmer.

Driscoll, W. (2005, July). *Peak performance under pressure.* Presentation at the McREL Summer Conference, Denver, CO.

DuFour, R., Eaker, R., & DuFour, R. (Eds.). (2005). *On common ground: The power of professional learning communities.* Bloomington, IN: Solution Tree (formerly National Educational Service).

DuFour, R., & Marzano, R. J. (2009). High-leverage strategies for principal leadership. *Educational Leadership, 66*(5), 62–69.

Durlak, J. A., & Weissberg, R. P. (2007). *The impact of after-school programs that seek to promote personal and social skills.* Chicago: Collaborative for Academic, Social, and Emotional Learning.

Elmore, R. (2003). *Knowing the right thing to do: School improvement and performance-based accountability.* Washington, DC: NGA Center for Best Practices.

Evans, D. F. (1994). A determination of organizational behavior within the context of three conceptual organizational models. *Dissertation Abstracts International, 57*(03), 943A. (UMI No. 9621710)

Fan, X. (2003). Two approaches for correction correlation attenuation caused by measurement error: Implications for research practice. *Educational and Psychological Measurement, 63*(6), 915–930.

Fantini, M. D. (1975). *The people and their schools: Community participation. Fastback, 62.* Bloomington, IN: Phi Delta Kappa Education Foundation.

Ferguson, P., & Womack, S. T. (1993). The impact of subject matter and education coursework on teaching performance. *Journal of Teacher Education, 44*(1), 55–63.

Ferguson, R. F. (1991, Summer). Paying for public education: New evidence on how and why money matters. *Harvard Journal on Legislation, 28*(2), 465–498.

Flinders, D. J. (1988). Teacher isolation and the new reform. *Journal of Curriculum and Supervision, 4*(1), 17–29.

The Forum. (1988). *North Carolina's lead teacher/restructured school pilot project: An interim report.* Raleigh, NC: Public School Forum of North Carolina.

Frieri, P. (1970). *The pedagogy of the oppressed* (M. B. Ramos, Trans.). New York: Herder & Herder.

Fuchs, L. S., & Fuchs, D. (1986). Effects of systematic formative evaluation: A meta analysis. *Exceptional Children, 53*(3), 199–208.

Fullan, M. (1993). *Change forces: Probing the depths of educational reform*. London: Falmer.

Fullan, M. (2001). *The new meaning of educational change* (3rd ed.). New York and London: Teachers College Press and RoutledgeFalmer.

Gladwell, M. (2002). *The tipping point: How little things can make a big difference*. Boston: Little, Brown.

Glass, G. V. (1976). Primary, secondary and meta-analysis of research. *Educational Researcher, 5*(10), 3–8.

Glass, G. V. (1977). Integrating findings: The meta-analysis of research. *Review of Research in Education, 5*, 351–379.

Glass, T. E., Bjork, L., & Brunner, C. C. (2000). *The study of the American school superintendency*. Arlington, VA: American Association of School Administrators.

Glassman, R. B. (1973). Persistence and loose coupling in living systems. *Behavioral Science, 18*, 83–98.

Goddard, R. D., Hoy, W. K., & Hoy, A. W. (2004). Collective efficacy beliefs: Theoretical developments, empirical evidence, and future directions. *Educational Researcher, 33*(3), 3–13.

Gonzales, P. (2004). *Highlights from trends in international mathematics and science study (TIMSS), 2003*. Washington, DC: National Center for Education Statistics, U.S. Department of Education.

Good, T. L., & Brophy, J. E. (2003). *Looking in classrooms* (9th ed.). Boston: Allyn & Bacon.

Goodlad, J. I. (1984). *A place called school*. New York: McGraw-Hill.

Goodlad, J. I. (1995). *Educational renewal*. San Francisco: Jossey-Bass.

Green, R. L., & Etheridge, C. P. (2005). Collaborating to establish standards and accountability: Lessons learned about systemic change. *Education, 121*(4), 821–829.

Greenwald, R., Hedges, L. V., & Laine, R. D. (1996a). The effect of school resources on student achievement. *Review of Educational Research, 66*(3), 361–396.

Greenwald, R., Hedges, L. V., & Laine, R. D. (1996b). Interpreting research on school resources and student achievement: A rejoinder to Hanushek. *Review of Educational Research, 66*(3), 411–416.

Guilfoyle, C. (2006). NCLB: Is there life beyond testing? *Educational Leadership, 64*(3), 8–13.

Hall, G. E., & Hord, S. M. (1987). *Change in schools: Facilitating the process*. Albany: State University of New York Press.

Hall, G. E., & Loucks, S. F. (1978). A developmental model for determining whether the treatment is actually implemented. *American Educational Research Journal, 14*(3), 263–270.

Hall, G. E., Loucks, S. F., Rutherford, W. L., & Newlove, B. W. (1975). Levels of use of the innovation: A framework for analyzing innovation adoption. *Journal of Teacher Education, 26*(1), 52–56.

Haney, W., Madaus, G., & Kreitzer, A. (1987). Charms talismanic: Testing teachers for the improvement of American education. In E. Z. Rothkopf (Ed.), *Review of research in education* (Vol. 14, pp. 169–238). Washington, DC: American Educational Research Association.

Hanushek, E. A. (1981). Throwing money at schools. *Journal of Policy Analysis and Management, 1,* 19–41.

Hanushek, E. A. (1986). The economics of schooling: Production and efficiency in public schools. *Journal of Economic Literature, 25,* 1141–1177.

Hanushek, E. A. (1989). The impact of differential expenditures on school performance. *Educational Researcher, 18*(4), 45–62.

Hanushek, E. A. (1991). When school finance "reform" may not be good policy. *Harvard Journal on Legislation, 28,* 423–456.

Hanushek, E. A. (with others). (1994). *Making schools work: Improving performance and controlling costs.* Washington, DC: Brookings Institution.

Hanushek, E. A. (1996). A more complete picture of school resources policies. *Review of Educational Research, 66*(3), 397–409.

Hardy, L. (2007, November). The value of collaboration: To avoid takeovers, school districts must learn to collaborate with city leaders. *American School Board Journal, 94*(11), 38–39.

Hattie, J. (1984). An empirical study of various indices for determining unidimensionality. *Multivariate Behavioral Research, 19,* 49–78.

Hattie, J. (1985). Methodology review: Assessing the unidimensionality of tests and items. *Applied Psychological Measurement, 9*(2), 139–164.

Hauser, R. M. (1972). *Socioeconomic background and educational performance.* Washington, DC: American Sociological Association.

Haycock, K. (1998). Good teaching matters…a lot. *Thinking K–16, 3*(2), 1–14.

Heath, C., & Heath, D. (2007). *Made to stick: Why some ideas survive and others die.* New York: Random House.

Hedges, L. V., Laine, R. D., & Greenwald, R. (1994). Does money matter? A meta-analysis of studies on the effects of differential school inputs on student outcomes. *Educational Researcher, 23*(3), 5–14.

Hedges, L. V., & Nowell, A. (1999). Changes in the Black–White gap in test scores. *Sociology of Education, 72,* 111–135.

Hedges, L. V., & Olkin, I. (1985). *Statistical methods for meta-analysis.* Orlando, FL: Academic Press.

Heifetz, R. A. (1994). *Leadership without easy answers.* Cambridge, MA: Belknap Press of Harvard University Press.

Hill, H. C. (2007). Mathematical knowledge of middle school teachers: Implications for the No Child Left Behind policy initiative. *Educational Evaluation and Policy Analysis, 29*(2), 95–114.

Hord, S. M. (1997). *Professional learning communities: Communities of continuous inquiry and improvement.* Austin, TX: Southwest Educational Development Laboratory.

Hord, S. M. (2004). Professional learning communities: An overview. In S. M. Hord (Ed.), *Learning together, leading together: Changing schools through professional learning communities* (pp. 5–14). New York: Teachers College Press.

Hord, S. M., Rutherford, W. L., Huling-Austin, L., & Hall, G. E. (1987). *Taking charge of change.* Alexandria, VA: Association for Supervision and Curriculum Development.

Howell, W. (Ed.). (2005). *Besieged: School boards and the future of education politics.* Washington, DC: Brookings Institution.

Hunter, J. E., & Schmidt, F. L. (1990). Methods of meta-analysis: Correcting error and bias in research findings. (1st ed.). Newbury Park, CA: Sage.

Hunter, J. E., & Schmidt, F. L. (1994). Correcting for sources of artifactual variance across studies. In H. Cooper & L. V. Hedges (Eds.), *Handbook of research synthesis* (pp. 323–338). New York: Russell Sage.

Hunter, J. E., & Schmidt, F. L. (2004). *Methods of meta-analysis: Correcting error and bias in research findings.* Thousand Oaks, CA: Sage.

Hunter, M. (1984). Knowing, teaching, and supervising. In P. Hosford (Ed.), *Using what we know about teaching* (pp. 169–192). Alexandria, VA: Association for Supervision and Curriculum Development.

Institute for Educational Leadership. (2001). *Leadership for student learning: Restructuring school district leadership.* Washington, DC: Author.

Jacobsen, J., Olsen, C., Rice, J. K., Sweetland, S., & Ralph, J. (2001). *Educational achievement and Black–White inequality.* Washington, DC: National Center for Education Statistics, U.S. Department of Education.

Jenkins, J. R., Ronk, J., Schrag, J. A., Rude, G. C., & Stowitschek, C. (1994). Effects of school-based participatory decision making to improve services for low-performing students. *Elementary School Journal, 94*(3), 357–372.

Kerr, R. P. (1988, December). Superintendents best serve their schools by staying put. *Executive Educator, 20*–21.

King, M. B., & Newmann, F. M. (2001). Building school capacity through professional development: Conceptual and empirical considerations. *International Journal of Educational Management, 15*(2), 86–93.

Kozol, J. (1992). *Savage inequalities: Children in America's schools.* New York: HarperCollins.

Ladewig, B. G. (2006). *The minority achievement gap in New York State suburban schools since the implementation of NCLB.* Unpublished doctoral dissertation, University of Rochester, New York.

Land, D. (2002). *Local school boards under review: Their role and effectiveness in relation to students' academic achievement.* Baltimore: Johns Hopkins University, Center for Research on the Education of Students Placed at Risk.

Lauer, P. A., Akiba, M., Wilkerson, S. B., Apthorp, H. S., Snow, D., & Martin-Glenn, M. L. (2006). Out-of-school-time programs: A meta-analysis of effects for at-risk students. *Review of Educational Research, 76*(2), 275–313.

Lipsey, M. W., & Wilson, D. B. (2001). *Practical meta-analysis.* Thousand Oaks, CA: Sage.

Little, J. W. (2002). Locating learning in teachers' communities of practice: Opening up problems of analysis in records of everyday work. *Teaching and Teacher Education, 18*(8), 917–946.

Lou, Y., Abrami, P. C., Spence, J. C., Poulsen, C., Chambers, B., & d'Apollonia, S. (1996). Within-class grouping: A meta-analysis. *Review of Educational Research, 66*(4), 423–458.

Louis, K. S., Kruse, S. D., & Associates. (1995). *Professionalism and community: Perspectives on reforming urban schools.* Thousand Oaks, CA: Corwin Press.

Magnusson, D. (1966). *Test theory.* Reading, MA: Addison-Wesley.

Malen, B., Ogawa, R. T., & Kranz, J. (1990a). Site-based management: Unfulfilled promises. *School Administrator, 42*(2), 3–56.

Malen, B., Ogawa, R. T., & Kranz, J. (1990b). What do we know about school-based management? A case study of the literature—a call for research. In W. H. Clune & J. F. Witte (Eds.), *Choice and control in American education Volume 2: The practice of choice, decentralization and school restructuring* (pp. 289–342). New York: Falmer.

Marzano & Associates. (2005). *Blue Springs School District instructional strategies project: Final report.* Centennial, CO: Author.

Marzano, R. J. (2002). A comparison of selected methods of scoring classroom assessments. *Applied Measurement in Education, 15*(3), 249–268.

Marzano, R. J. (2003). *What works in schools: Translating research into action.* Alexandria, VA: Association for Supervision and Curriculum Development.

Marzano, R. J. (2006). *Classroom assessment and grading that work.* Alexandria, VA: Association for Supervision and Curriculum Development.

Marzano, R. J. (2007a). Designing a comprehensive approach to classroom assessment. In D. Reeves (Ed.), *Ahead of the curve: The power of assessment to transform teaching and learning* (pp. 103–126). Bloomington, IN: Solution Tree.

Marzano, R. J. (2007b). *The art and science of teaching.* Alexandria, VA: Association for Supervision and Curriculum Development.

Marzano, R. J. (2007c). Using action research and local models of instruction to enhance teaching. *Journal of Personnel Evaluation in Education, 20*(3/4), 117–128.

Marzano, R. J. (2008). *Getting serious about school reform.* Centennial, CO: Marzano & Associates.

Marzano, R. J. (2009). Formative versus summative assessments as measures of student learning. In T. J. Kowalski & T. J. Lashley III (Eds.), *Handbook of data-based decision making in education* (pp. 259–271). New York: Taylor & Francis.

Marzano, R. J., & Haystead, M. W. (2008). *Making standards useful in the classroom.* Alexandria, VA: Association for Supervision and Curriculum Development.

Marzano, R. J., Kendall, J. S., & Cicchinelli, L. F. (1998). *What Americans believe students should know: A survey of U.S. adults.* Aurora, CO: Mid-continent Regional Education Laboratory.

Marzano, R. J., Kendall, J. S., & Gaddy, B. B. (1999). *Essential knowledge: The debate over what American students should know.* Aurora, CO: Mid-continent Regional Education Laboratory.

Marzano, R. J., Pickering, D. J., & Marzano, J. S. (2003). *Classroom management that works: Research-based strategies for every teacher.* Alexandria, VA: Association for Supervision and Curriculum Development.

Marzano, R. J., Pickering, D. J., & Pollock, J. E. (2001). *Classroom instruction that works: Research-based strategies for increasing student achievement.* Alexandria, VA: Association for Supervision and Curriculum Development.

Marzano, R. J., Waters, T., & McNulty, B. A. (2005). *School leadership that works: From research to results.* Alexandria, VA: Association for Supervision and Curriculum Development.

Mayer, R. E. (2003). *Learning and instruction.* Upper Saddle River, NJ: Merrill, Prentice Hall.

McKinsey & Company. (2007). *How the world's best performing school systems come out on top.* New York: Author.

McMillan, J. H. (2007). Formative assessment: The key to improving student achievement. In J. H. McMillan (Ed.), *Formative classroom assessment: Theory into practice* (pp. 1–7). New York: Teachers College Press.

Meyer, J., & Rowan, B. (1978). The structure of educational organizations. In M. Meyer (Ed.), *Environments and organizations* (pp. 78–109). San Francisco: Jossey-Bass.

Miller, E. (1995, November/December). Shared decision-making by itself doesn't make for better decisions. *Harvard Education Newsletter.* Accessed at http://www.subscriber.edletter.org/past/1995-nd/sitebased.shtml on September 12, 2006.

Millman, J. (Ed.). (1997). *Grading teachers, grading schools: Is student achievement a valid evaluation measure?* Thousand Oaks, CA: Corwin Press.

Mitchell, C., & Sackney, L. (2000). *Profound improvement: Building capacity for a learning community.* Lisse, the Netherlands: Swets & Zeitlinger.

Monk, D. H. (1994). Subject matter preparation of secondary mathematics and science teachers and student achievement. *Economics of Education Review, 13*(2), 125–145.

Mullis, I. V. S., Martin, M. O., Beaton, A. E., Gonzalez, E. J., Kelly, D. L., & Smith, T. A. (1998). *TIMSS mathematics and science achievement in the final year of secondary school: IEA's third international mathematics and science of study.* Chestnut Hill, MA: Center for the Study of Testing, Evaluation, and Educational Policy, International Association for the Evaluation of Educational Achievement.

Mullis, I. V. S., Martin, M. O., Gonzalez, E. J., & Chrostowski, S. J. (2004a). *TIMSS 2003 international mathematics report.* Boston: Boston College, Lynch School of Education.

Mullis, I. V. S., Martin, M. O., Gonzalez, E. J., & Chrostowski, S. J. (2004b). *TIMSS 2003 international science report: Findings from IEA's trends in international mathematics and science and science study at the fourth and eighth grades.* Chestnut Hill, MA: Boston College.

Mullis, I. V. S., Martin, M. O., Gonzalez, E. J., & Chrostowski, S. J. (2004c). *TIMSS 2003 international mathematics report: Findings from IEA's trends in international mathematics and science study at the fourth and eighth grades.* Chestnut Hill, MA: Boston College.

National Center for Education Statistics. (NCES). (2008). *Fast facts.* Accessed at http://nces.ed.gov/fastfacts/display.asp?id=372 on August 2, 2008.

National Commission on Excellence in Education. (1983). *A nation at risk: The imperative for educational reform.* Washington, DC: U.S. Government Printing Office.

National Commission on Teaching and America's Future. (1998). *What matters most: Teaching for America's future.* New York: Author.

National Institute on Student Achievement, Curriculum, and Assessment; Office of Educational Research and Improvement; U.S. Department of Education. (1998). *The educational system in*

Japan: Case study findings. Accessed at http://www.ed.gov/pubs/JapanCaseStudy/title.html on September 24, 2008.

National Institute on Student Achievement, Curriculum, and Assessment; Office of Educational Research and Improvement; U.S. Department of Education. (1999). *The educational system in Germany: Case study findings.* Accessed at http://www.ed.gov/PDFDocs/GermanCaseStudy.pdf on September 24, 2008.

National Research Council. (1996). *National science education standards.* Washington, DC: National Academies Press.

No Child Left Behind Act of 2001, Pub. L. No. 107-110, 115 Stat. 1425 (2002).

Nolen, A. L., & Putten, J. V. (2007). Action research in education: Addressing gaps in ethical principles and practices. *Educational Researcher, 36*(7), 401–407.

Nye, B., Konstantopoulos, S., & Hedges, L. V. (2004). How large are teacher effects? *Educational Evaluation and Policy Analysis, 26*(3), 237–257.

Ohio Department of Education. (2001). *Academic content standards: K–12 mathematics.* Columbus, OH: Author.

Olson, L. (1995, June 14). Cards on the table. *Education Week,* 23–28.

Osborne, J. W. (2003). Effect sizes and the disattentuation of correlation and regression coefficients: Lessons from educational psychology. *Practical Assessment, Research and Evaluation, 8*(11). Accessed at http://PAREonline.net/getvn.asp?v=8&n=11 on March 19, 2009.

Palardy, G. J., & Rumberger, R. W. (2008). Teacher effectiveness in first grade: The importance of background qualifications, attitudes, and instructional practices for student learning. *Educational Evaluation and Policy Analysis, 30*(2), 111–140.

Parker, B. (1979, July). School-based management: Improve education by giving parents, principals more control of your schools. *American School Board Journal, 166*(7), 20–21, 24.

Plecki, M. L., McCleery, J., & Knapp, M. S. (2006). *Redefining and improving school district governance.* Seattle: University of Washington, Center for the Study of Teaching and Policy.

Popham, W. J. (2006). Phony formative assessments: Buyer beware. *Educational Leadership, 64*(3), 86–87.

Prentice, D. A., & Miller, D. T. (1992). When small effects are impressive. *Psychological Bulletin, 112*(1), 160–164.

Reeves, D. B. (2008). *Reframing teacher leadership: To improve your school.* Alexandria, VA: Association for Supervision and Curriculum Development.

Reynolds, D., & Teddlie, C. (with Hopkins, D., & Stringfield, S.). (2000). Linking school effectiveness and school improvement. In C. Teddlie & D. Reynolds (Eds.), *The international handbook of school effectiveness research* (pp. 206–231). New York: Falmer.

Robinson, V. M. J. (2007). *School leadership and student outcomes: Identifying what works and why.* Winmalee, NSW, Australia: Australian Council for Educational Leadership.

Rogers, E. M. (2003). *Diffusion of innovations* (5th ed.). New York: Free Press.

Rosenthal, R. (1984). *Meta-analysis procedures for social research.* Beverly Hills, CA: Sage.

Rosenthal, R. (1991). *Meta-analysis procedures for social research* (2nd ed.). Newbury Park, CA: Sage.

Rosenthal, R., & Rubin, D. B. (1982). A simple general purpose display of magnitude of experimental effects. *Journal of Educational Psychology, 74*(2), 166–169.

Roza, M. (2005). *Many a slip 'tween cup and lip: District fiscal practices and their effect on school spending.* Seattle: University of Washington, Center on Reinventing Public Education.

Sampson, P. M. (1999). Models of site-based management and parent perception of student achievement: A national study. *Dissertation Abstracts International, 60*(11), 3863A. (UMI No. 9950116)

Schalock, D. (1979). Research on teacher selection. In D. C. Berliner (Ed.), *Review of research in education* (Vol. 7, pp. 364–417). Washington, DC: American Educational Research Association.

Sell, S. (2006). Running an effective school district: School boards in the 21st century. *Journal of Education, 186*(3), 71–97.

Sen, A., Partelow, L., & Miller, D. C. (2005). *Comparative indicators of education in the United States and other G8 countries: 2004* (NCES 2005-021). U.S. Department of Education, National Center for Education Statistics. Washington, DC: U.S. Government Printing Office.

Shepard, L. (2006, June 26). Panelist presentation delivered at the National Large-Scale Assessment Conference sponsored by the Council of Chief State School Officers, San Francisco, CA.

Shulman, L. S. (2004). *Teaching as community property: Essays on higher education.* San Francisco: Jossey-Bass.

Sickler, J. L. (1988, January). Teachers in charge: Empowering the professionals. *Phi Delta Kappan, 69,* 354–356.

Snijders, T., & Bosker, R. (1999). *Multilevel analysis: An introduction to basic and advanced multilevel modeling.* Thousand Oaks, CA: Sage.

Soar, R. S., Medley, D. M., & Coker, H. (1983). Teacher evaluation: A critique of currently used methods. *Phi Delta Kappan, 65*(4), 239–246.

Stevenson, H. W., & Stigler, J. W. (1992). *The learning gap: Why our schools are failing and what we can learn from Japanese and Chinese education.* New York: Simon & Schuster.

Stigler, J. W., & Hiebert, J. (1999). *The teaching gap: Best ideas from the world's teachers for improving education in the classroom.* New York: Free Press.

Stoll, L., Bolam, R., McMahon, A., Wallace, M., & Thomas, S. (2006). Professional learning communities: A review of the literature. *Journal of Educational Change, 7,* 221–258.

Thomas, M. D. (1980). Parent participation in education. *NASSP Bulletin, 64,* 1–3.

Toole, J. C., & Louis, K. S. (2002). The role of professional learning communities in international education. In K. Leithwood and P. Hallinger (Eds.), *Second international handbook of educational leadership and administration* (pp. 245–279). Dordrecht, the Netherlands: Kluwer.

Tucker, P. D., & Stronge, J. H. (2005). *Linking teacher evaluation and student learning.* Alexandria, VA: Association for Supervision and Curriculum Development.

U.S. Department of Education. (2002). *Meeting the highly qualified teachers challenge: The secretary's annual report on teacher quality.* Washington, DC: U.S. Department of Education, Office of Postsecondary Education.

Walker, R. (1987, March 2). Bennett: Test gains at a "dead stall." *Education Week, 7*(23), 5.

Ward, M. (2007, March). For schools to be successful, boards and administrators must engage leaders at all levels. *American School Board Journal,* 26–29.

Warner-King, K., & Smith-Casem, V. (2005). *Addressing funding inequalities within districts.* Seattle: University of Washington, Center on Reinventing Public Education.

Weglinsky, H. (2000). *How teachers matter: Bringing the classroom back into discussions of teacher quality.* Princeton, NJ: Educational Testing Service.

Weick, K. E. (1976). Educational organizations as loosely coupled systems. *Administrative Science Quarterly, 21*(1), 1–19.

Weick, K. E. (1982). Administering education in a loosely coupled system. *Phi Delta Kappan, 63*(10), 673–676.

Weick, K. E., Sutcliffe, K., & Obstfeld, D. (1999). Organizing for high reliability: Process of collective mindfulness. *Research in Organizational Behavior, 21,* 81–123.

Weiss, C. (1995, Winter). The four "I's" of school reform: How interests, ideology, information, and institution affect teachers and principals. *Harvard Educational Review, 65*(4), 571–592.

Wiley, D., & Yoon, B. (1995). Teacher reports of opportunity to learn: Analyses of the 1993 California learning assessment system. *Educational Evaluation and Policy Analysis, 17*(3), 355–370.

Wiliam, D., & Leahy, S. (2007). A theoretical foundation for formative assessment. In J. H. McMillan (Ed.), *Formative classroom assessment: Theory into practice* (pp. 29–42). New York: Teachers College Press.

Willms, J. D. (1992). *Monitoring school performance: A guide for educators.* Washington, DC: Falmer.

Wynn, R. (1983). *Collective bargaining: An alternative to conventional bargaining. Fastback, 185.* Bloomington, IN: Phi Delta Kappa Education Foundation.

Zellmer, M. B., Frontier, A., & Pheifer, D. (2006). What are NCLB's instructional costs? *Educational Leadership, 64*(3), 43–46.

Index

A

AASA. *See* American Association of School
    Administrators
Abelson (1985), 129
Abrams (2007), 26
acceptance of new ideas, using what is known about,
    110–111
accountability
allocating resources, 79
    context for achievement goals, 25–27
    formative assessments research, 29
    high-reliability organization evidence, 19
    history of school boards, 76–77
    second-order change, 106
achievement goals
    monitoring. *See* monitoring of goals for
        achievement
    setting. *See* ensuring collaborative goal setting;
        setting nonnegotiable goals for achievement
    support for. *See* allocating resources to support
        goals; creating board alignment and support
achievement tests. *See* testing
action research, instructional strategies exploration,
    57–59
active forms of learning, 45–46
administrator/district leadership relations, 109–113
administrator observation of teachers, 66, 68–69
administrator perspective on organizations, 14, 18
adoption of innovations, using what is known about,
    110–111
advice for district leaders
    communicating with sticky messages, 111–112
    epilogue, 116
    keeping big ideas in forefront, 110
    knowing implications of initiatives, 109
    maintaining unified front, 109–110
    managing personal transitions, 112–113
    using what is known about acceptance, 110–111
AERA database, 3
affirmation responsibility, 92, 94, 98, 99, 101
after-school programs, 43–48
Alexander (1976), 136
allocating resources to support goals
    costs of assessment, 26
    findings of study, 77–85
    interaction of findings, 23–24, 71–72
    measure of inequality, 84

overview of study, 6, 8, 12
putting findings in perspective, 21–22
school leadership for defined autonomy, 94, 99–102
second-order change, 105, 107
summary, 85
technical notes, 129, 131
American Association of School Administrators, 113
art achievement, 48, 51
artifacts, correcting for, 3, 118–120
Ashton and Crocker (1987), 55
assessments. *See* formative assessments; summative
    assessments; testing
"associated with" terminology, 117–118
attendance, school outcomes meta-analysis, 46
attenuation artifacts, correcting for, 3, 118–120
Australia, effective schools study, 20
autonomy. *See* defined autonomy; school autonomy

B

background of study, 1–2
Baker and LeTendre (2005), 18, 83–84
Barton (2006), 27
batting average variance example, 129
Baugh (2002), 120
behavioral adjustments outcomes category, 46
Belgium, effective schools study, 20
beliefs and failure of societies, 115
Bellamy, Crawford, Marshall, and Coulter (2005),
    19–20
benchmark assessments, 29–30, 116. *See also* forma-
    tive assessments
Bennett, Finn, and Cribb (1999), 1
Bennett, William, 1, 9
between-classes variance component, 133–134
between-school variance component, 133–138
big ideas, keeping in forefront, 110
binomial effect size display, technical notes, 126–129
biological diversity and evolution of life, scale for,
    35–36, 39–40
Black and Wiliam (1998), 27–30
blob (bloated educational bureaucracy), 1–2, 9
The Blob (movie), 1
boards, school. *See* creating board alignment and
    support; school boards
bonus finding
    overview of study, 9
    revisiting the finding, 113–114

Reeves (2008), 57, 58, 59
reform. *See* school reform
relationships responsibility, 92, 100, 101
relative advantage attribute, 110
reliability of dependent measure, as moderator variable, 121–122
reliability of independent measure, as moderator variable, 122
reliability of test scores, 26–27, 119
report cards, 48–52, 77, 106, 109–113
reporting systems, status-oriented, 25–27, 28, 52. *See also* summative assessments
reporting topics, in formative assessments. *See* formative assessments
research questions overview, 2, 4–9
resilience, inspiring, 99
resource allocation. *See* allocating resources to support goals
resource availability, change as relative to, 105, 107
resources responsibility, 91, 94, 100
Robinson (2007), 90
Rogers (2003), 110
Rosenthal (1984), 118
Rosenthal (1991), 118
Rosenthal and Rubin (1982), 127–128
Roza (2005), 84–85

S

salaries, 78, 80–81
Sampson (1999), 16
scales for formative assessments
  biological diversity and evolution of life, 35–36, 39–40
  generic scale, 34
  pedagogical skills improvement and, 63, 64
  summary, 52
school autonomy. *See also* defined autonomy
  common work of schools, 89–90
  overview of study, 8–9
  putting findings in perspective, 18
  technical notes, 131–132
school-based management. *See* site-based management
school boards
  alignment with goals. *See* creating board alignment and support
  collaborative goal setting and, 6, 74
  history of, 75–77
  monitoring nonnegotiable goals, 98
  superintendent tenure, 114
school failures, addressing, 99
school-generated reports, 42–43
school leadership and competence as factor. *See also specific aspects*
  leadership findings comparison, 87–89
  leadership for defined autonomy, 90–103
  overview of study, 9–11, 12
  second-order change, 107–108

technical notes, 132–138
school performance outcomes category, 46
school reform
  allocating resources, 79, 82
  comprehensive reform models, 114
  history of school boards, 76–77
  interaction of findings, 23–24
  site-based management significance, 16
  worldwide effective schools study, 20–21
school report cards, 77
school successes, addressing, 99
school superintendents. *See* superintendents
science achievement
  allocating resources, 80, 83
  context for achievement goals, 25
  effective schools study, 20
  high-quality teacher characteristics, 56
  reconstituting state standards, 31–33, 35–36
  report card redesign, 48–49
  tracking student progress, 39–40
second-order change
  advice for district leaders, 109–113
  background, 105–107
  bonus finding revisited, 113–114
  living through tough times, 107–109
Sell (2006), 74, 77
sequenced training strategies, 45–46
setting nonnegotiable goals for achievement
  background, 23–24
  characteristics of formatively based, value-added system, 29–30
  context for, 24–27
  interaction of findings, 23–24, 71–72
  need for formatively based, value-added system, 27–29
  overview of study, 6–7, 12
  providing support for students, 43–48
  putting findings in perspective, 18, 21–22
  reconstituting state standards, 30–38
  redesigning report cards, 48–52, 106, 109–113
  school leadership for defined autonomy, 94, 96–97
  second-order change, 105–114
  summary, 52
  technical notes, 129, 130
  tracking student progress, 39–43
setting nonnegotiable goals for instruction
  background, 53–54
  characteristics of high-quality teachers, 54–56
  continuous improvement as goal, 56–57
  designing a model or language, 60–61
  exploring and examining strategies, 57–60
  interacting with other teachers, 62–63
  interaction of findings, 23–24, 71–72
  monitoring effectiveness of styles, 65–70
  observing other teachers, 63–65
  overview of study, 6–7, 12
  putting findings in perspective, 18, 21–22
  school leadership for defined autonomy, 94, 96–97

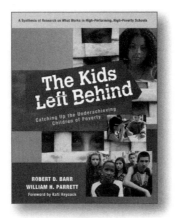
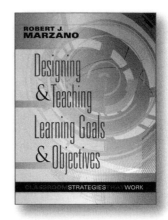

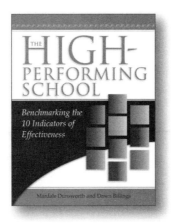
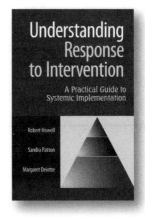

Solution Tree | Press

a division of

Solution Tree

Solution Tree's mission is to advance the work of our authors. By working with the best researchers and educators worldwide, we strive to be the premier provider of innovative publishing, in-demand events, and inspired professional development designed to transform education to ensure that all students learn.

Based in Denver, Colorado, McREL (Mid-continent Research for Education and Learning) is a nonprofit organization dedicated to its mission of making a difference in the quality of education and learning for all through excellence in applied research, product development, and service. For more than forty years, McREL has served as the federally funded regional educational laboratory for seven states in the U.S. heartland. Today, it provides services to an international audience of educators. Specifically, it offers a variety of services to help districts translate guidance from this book into results for students. To learn more, contact McREL at 1.800.781.0156 or info@mcrel.org.